This edition first published in 2021 by Gecko Press
PO Box 9335, Wellington 6141, New Zealand
info@geckopress.com

English-language edition © Gecko Press Ltd 2021
Translation © Daniel Hahn 2021

Original edition: *Les Animaux des Mondes Perdus*, Actes Sud, France, 2019

All rights reserved. No part of this publication may be reproduced or transmitted or utilized in any form, or by any means, electronic, mechanical, photocopying or otherwise without the prior written permission of the publisher.

This book is supported by the Institut Français (Royaume-Uni) as part of the Burgess programme.

Edited by Penelope Todd and Elizabeth Karre
Cover design by Spencer Levine
Typesetting by Esther Chua
Printed in China by Everbest Printing Co. Ltd, an accredited ISO 14001 & FSC-certified printer

ISBN: 978-1-776573-15-8

For more curiously good books, visit geckopress.com

FOSSILS FROM LOST WORLDS

Hélène Rajcak

Damien Laverdunt

Translated by
Daniel Hahn

GECKO PRESS

PREFACE

Far back in the distant past, some children find a strange pebble on a beach. It is shaped like a flattened snail. They show it to their parents, who don't seem to be listening because they're looking for a place to stay for the night. But then they begin to pay attention—these stone animals are highly sought after, so perhaps they could spend a day or two collecting. The children are some of the first collectors and many will come after them. Stones such as these will come to be used for decoration, gifts and currency.

Over the next hundreds of thousands of years, fossilized animals continue to be sought out, turned into cash, and collected. People add to their collections of treasures: horns of Ammon and unicorn horns, giants' bones and cyclops skulls. These objects show off their owners' wealth and power but also build interest in the past and in distant lands.

Over time, our taste for relics and fossils has not run dry. Collectors from prehistoric times, the scholars of yesterday, and today's scientists have much in common. Many of them have covered great distances, walking up and down beaches, mountainsides and lands that bear witness to the biodiversity we have lost. They all learn by diligent observation and meticulous examination from these rocks dug up from the depths of the Earth. They ask questions. What might this object be? Did giants and monsters populate the planet long ago? Did species once exist that are now extinct? What was life like before our own? What was life like when it first began?

Fossils from Lost Worlds draws us into the story of the amazing discoveries and the great questions about how life on our planet began and changed. It leads us enjoyably down the wrong paths taken by some researchers with overlarge imaginations or limited scientific knowledge. These stories let us walk in the footsteps of fossil hunters and relive scenes in history. They allow us as readers to solve the mystery of a reversed footprint, identify a giant taller than a house, uncover a skeleton with a neck as long as its tail and much more.

Cécile Fromont-Colin
Head of the Palaeontology and Comparative Anatomy Gallery
National Museum of Natural History, Paris

CONTENTS

7
PREFACE

10
TABLE OF GEOLOGICAL PERIODS

12
THE BEGINNINGS OF ANIMAL LIFE

14
What did the oldest animal on Earth look like?

DICKINSONIA
Mysterious organism from the earliest times

16
What ancient secret is hidden in the mountains at Burgess?

ANOMALOCARIS
The jigsaw puzzle fossil

18
How do you bring back a world that has disappeared?

HALLUCIGENIA
The creature without head or tail

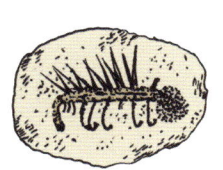

20
What is the real power of "snake stones"?

AMMONOIDEA
Collectors' fossils

22
How did fish learn to walk?

TIKTAALIK
The walking fish

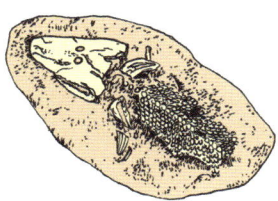

24
REIGN OF THE REPTILES

26
How was the mystery of the Thuringia footprints solved?

TICINOSUCHUS
A reptile unmasked

28
How did Mary Anning become a famous fossil-hunter?

PLESIOSAURUS
The peaceable dragon of the sea

30
Did chickens once have teeth?

ARCHAEOPTERYX
The oldest bird

32
How did *Diplodocus* become a celebrity?

DIPLODOCUS
The nimble colossus

34
Who won the bone wars?

STEGOSAURUS
The spiny giant of the Jurassic

36
How did "dinomania" begin?

IGUANODON
The dinosaur with "a thousand faces"

38
How did the ancestors of birds learn to fly?

MICRORAPTOR
The four-winged dinosaur

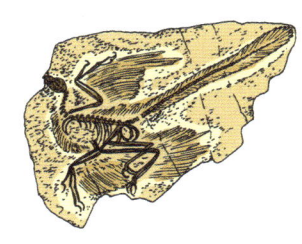

40
Did dinosaurs have scales, fur or feathers?

DEINONYCHUS
The new dinosaur

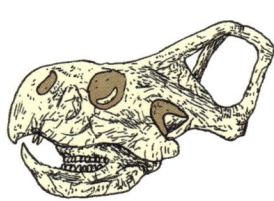

42
How do you draw a dinosaur?

PROTOCERATOPS
The herbivore of the Cretaceous

44
How was the "egg stealer" acquitted?

OVIRAPTOR
The mother-hen dinosaur

46
What was *Parasaurolophus*'s crest for?

PARASAUROLOPHUS
The tenor of extinct times

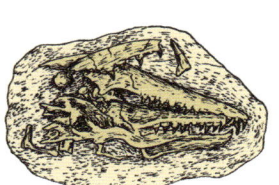

48
How was the monster of Maastricht revealed?

MOSASAURUS
The *T. rex* of the seas

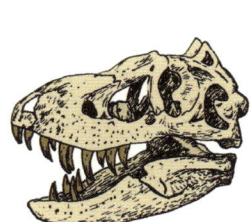

50
How did *T. rex* become a movie star?

TYRANNOSAURUS
The icon of vanished worlds

52

THE AGE OF MAMMALS AND BIRDS

54
How do you survive a mass extinction?

PURGATORIUS
The little survivor

56
What family secret is the whale hiding?

PAKICETUS
The whale with legs

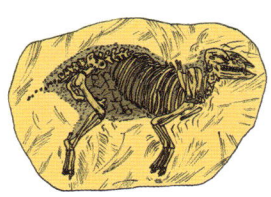

58
How were the Messel fossils preserved?

PROPALAEOTHERIUM
The miniature horse

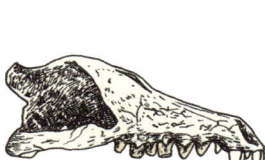

60
What fossil treasures were found in the Gobi Desert?

ANDREWSARCHUS
The enigmatic carnivore

62
What animals roamed the Badlands long, long ago?

MEGACEROPS
Hooves of thunder

64
How long did it take to uncover the behemoth of the Lost Valley?

PARACERATHERIUM
The last of the giants

66
A BRIEF HISTORY OF PALEONTOLOGY

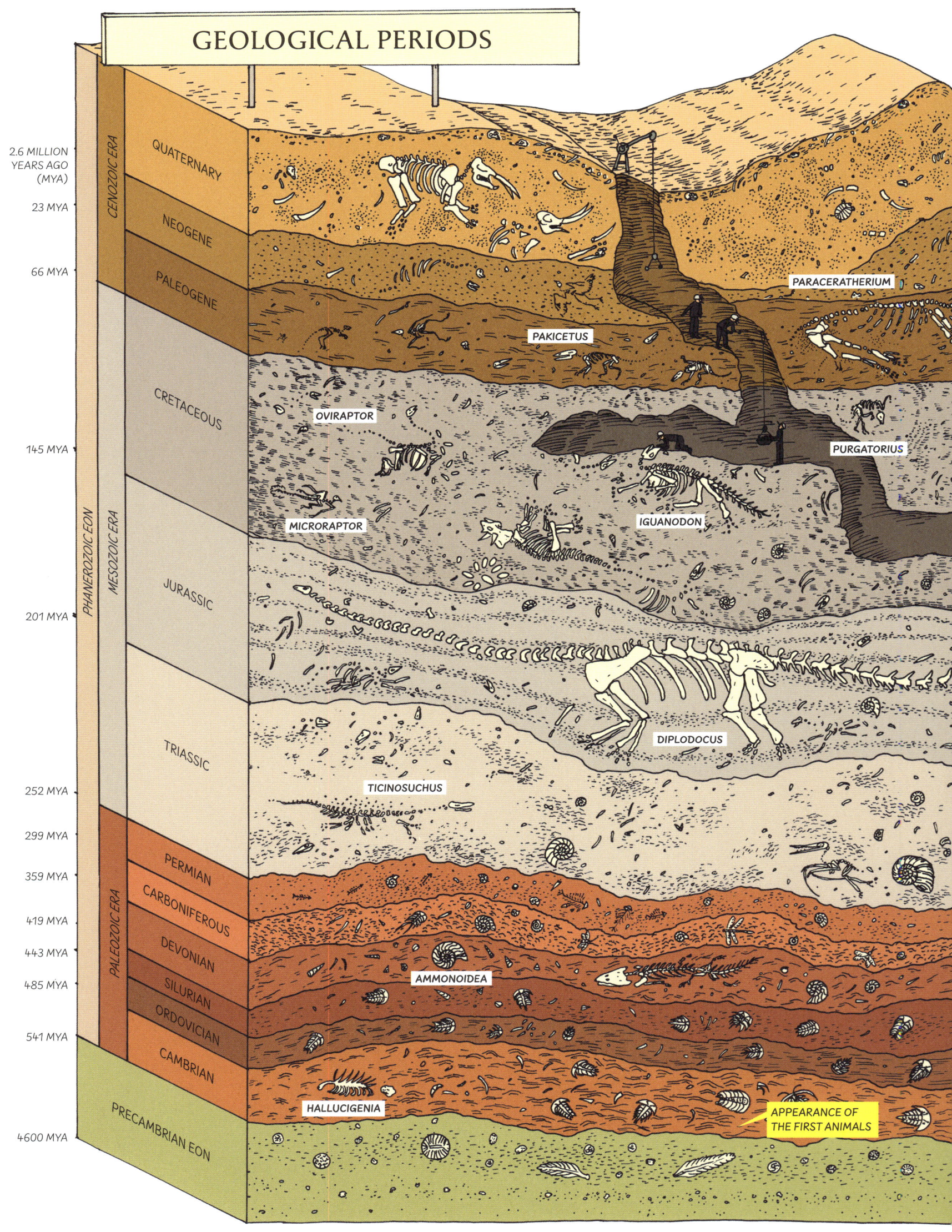

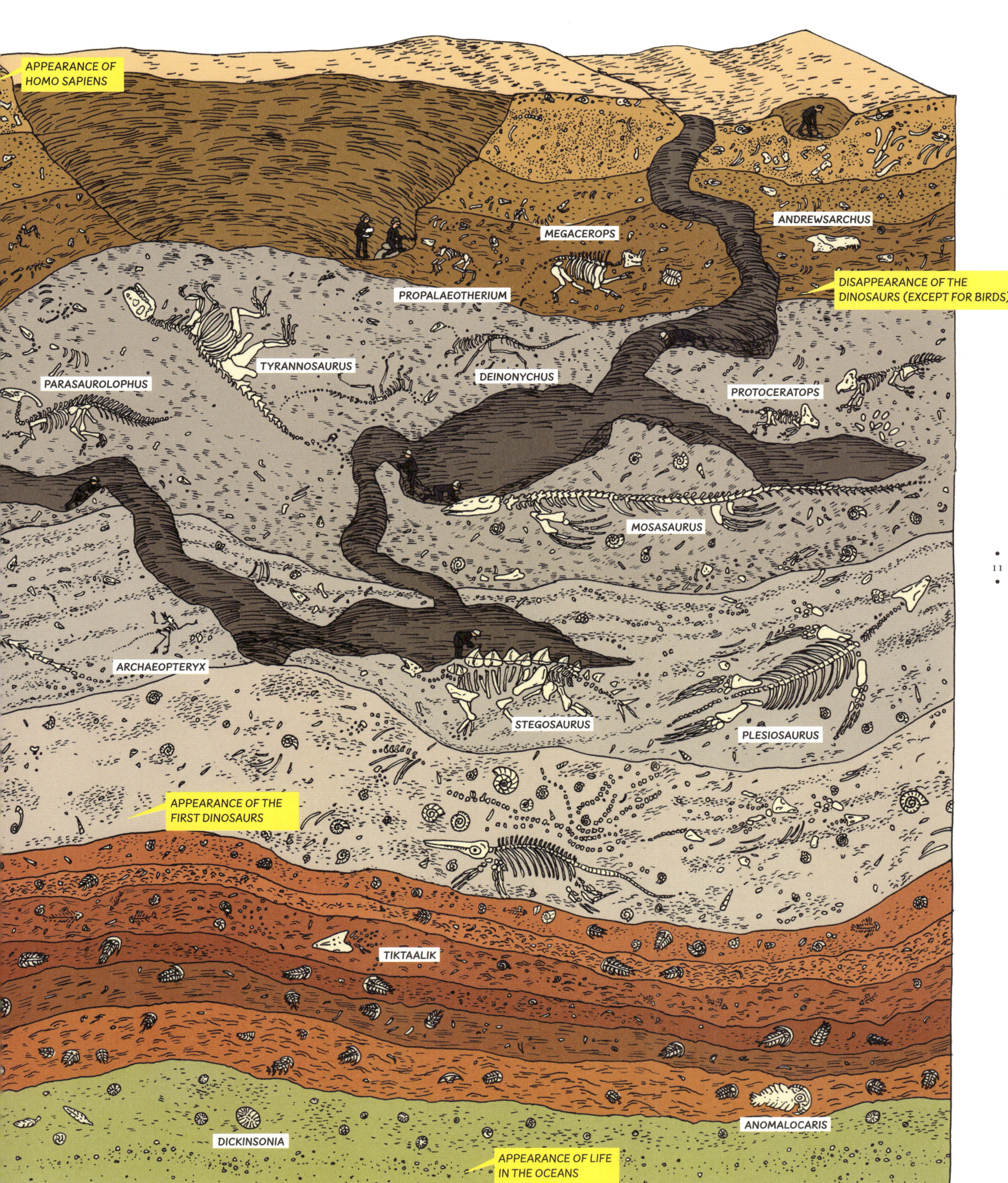

THE BEGINNINGS OF ANIMAL LIFE

To organize the 4.6 billion years of the Earth's history, geologists and paleontologists divide time into eras and periods. For a long time, the oldest fossils that had been identified by scientists were from the Paleozoic era, which covers the time from 541 to 252 million years ago. But more recently, people have identified even older fossils and realized that animal life on Earth began much earlier. This section begins by explaining how scientists learned about some of the first complex (multi-celled) organisms, like *Dickinsonia* and *Hallucigenia*. It moves on to the first animals with shells, such as ammonites (*Ammonoidea*), and ends with the first amphibians that came out of the water to live on land, like *Tiktaalik*.

WHAT DID THE OLDEST ANIMAL ON EARTH LOOK LIKE?

FOR PALEONTOLOGISTS, THE SEARCH FOR THE OLDEST ANIMAL FOSSIL IS VERY IMPORTANT FOR UNDERSTANDING HOW LIFE EVOLVED ON EARTH. AT FIRST, TRILOBITES AND THE CREATURES DISCOVERED AT THE START OF THE 20TH CENTURY (SEE P.16) WERE THOUGHT TO BE THE FIRST ANIMALS. BUT IN 1947, PALEONTOLOGISTS DISCOVERED EVIDENCE OF ANIMALS LIVING EVEN LONGER AGO IN THE HILLS OF EDIACARA IN SOUTH AUSTRALIA, DATING BACK APPROXIMATELY **560 MILLION YEARS**. THESE REMAIN THE OLDEST FOSSILIZED TRACKS TO DATE.

DOES THIS MEAN THAT THERE IS NO EVIDENCE OF EVEN OLDER LIFE? THERE ARE ROCKS THAT CONTAIN TRACES INVISIBLE TO THE NAKED EYE. WITH THE HELP OF MICROSCOPES AND CHEMICAL ANALYSIS, RESEARCHERS HAVE BEEN ABLE TO STUDY FOSSIL MOLECULES. THESE CHEMICAL TRACES LEFT BY LIVING CREATURES SUGGEST THAT OUR MOST DISTANT ANCESTOR MIGHT BE A LIVING SPONGE FROM MORE THAN **635 MILLION YEARS** AGO. OTHER EVIDENCE COULD PROVE THAT ANIMALS WERE ON EARTH AS LONG AS **800 MILLION YEARS** AGO. EARLIER STILL, THE REMAINS OF MULTICELLULAR ORGANISMS AND TRACES OF THEIR MOVEMENT HAVE BEEN RECORDED IN SEDIMENTS DATING BACK **2.1 BILLION YEARS**.

BUT THE RESEARCH INTO OUR ORIGINS DOESN'T STOP THERE! THE DISCOVERY AND STUDY OF STROMATOLITES, STRANGE FOSSIL STRUCTURES, HAVE MADE IT POSSIBLE TO TRACK THE FIRST SIGNS OF LIFE TO **3.5 BILLION YEARS** AGO. INSIDE THESE STONES, SCIENTISTS OBSERVED FOSSILIZED TRACES OF THE ACTIVITY OF GROUPS OF BACTERIA, SIMPLE LIFE FORMS. THESE MICROBE COMMUNITIES THAT LED TO THE CREATION OF STROMATOLITES RULED OVER MARINE LIFE FOR HUNDREDS OF MILLIONS OF YEARS. LATER, AS MORE COMPLEX LIFE FORMS, SUCH AS ANIMALS, CAME ON THE SCENE, THE MICROBE COMMUNITIES BECAME SMALLER.

DICKINSONIA
MYSTERIOUS ORGANISM FROM THE EARLIEST TIMES

Ever since fossils were discovered by a geologist in ancient mines in the Australian Ediacara hills, they have raised many doubts and a great deal of controversy.

Dickinsonia is one of these soft-bodied organisms that lived more than 550 million years ago, and its identification led to arguments. Different scientists compared it to jellyfish, worms, lichen or algae. Experts were unable to classify it, so a new animal family was created for it.

If recent studies prove that this was indeed an animal, we are still unsure how it is related to the animals we know today.

- Found in the Ediacara hills, Australia (1947)
- Up to 1.4 m long
- Lived 560 to 555 million years ago

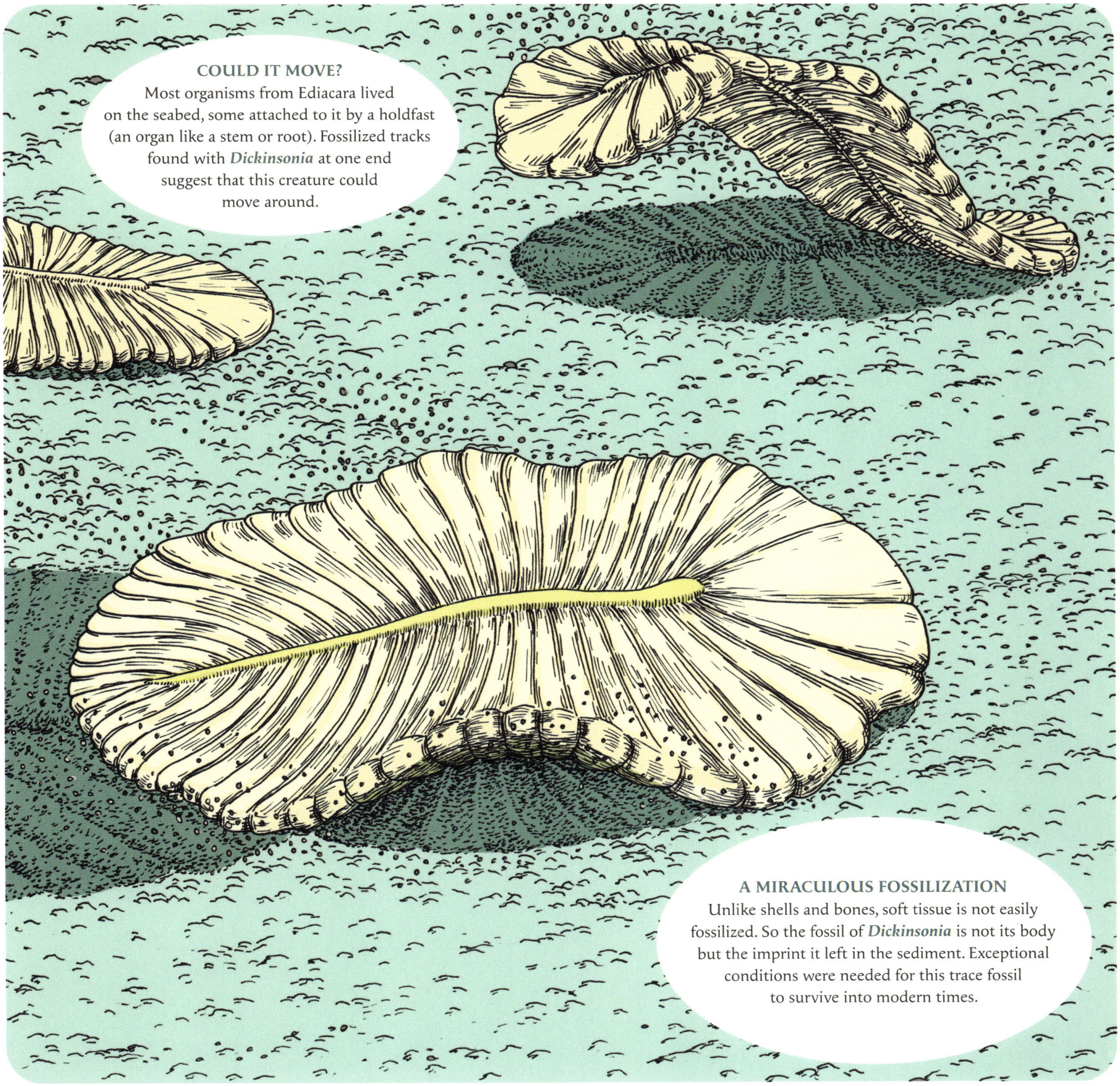

COULD IT MOVE?
Most organisms from Ediacara lived on the seabed, some attached to it by a holdfast (an organ like a stem or root). Fossilized tracks found with *Dickinsonia* at one end suggest that this creature could move around.

A MIRACULOUS FOSSILIZATION
Unlike shells and bones, soft tissue is not easily fossilized. So the fossil of *Dickinsonia* is not its body but the imprint it left in the sediment. Exceptional conditions were needed for this trace fossil to survive into modern times.

WHAT ANCIENT SECRET IS HIDDEN IN THE MOUNTAINS AT BURGESS?

ANOMALOCARIS
THE JIGSAW PUZZLE FOSSIL

As with many fossils, putting together the correct skeleton for *Anomalocaris* was like doing a jigsaw puzzle whose pieces turned up over time. First an isolated appendage of the animal was found in 1892. It was mistaken for the tail of an ancient shrimp. Then, at the start of the 20th century, Charles Walcott thought the animal's fossilized mouth was a jellyfish. Around the same time, a fossil of its body was mistaken for a sea cucumber. Finally in 1978 a complete fossil was found and scientists realized all the pieces went together to make a single animal. Although paleontologists today can agree on the appearance of *Anomalocaris*, they are still discussing how it behaved and whether it was a top predator.

- Found in Burgess, Canada (1892, identified as such in 1978)
- Up to 1 m long
- Lived 530 to 501 million years ago

COMPOUND EYES
A recently discovered fossil shows that *Anomalocaris* had compound eyes, like those of flies. These impressive, protruding eyes would have given it excellent vision for spotting its prey.

HUNTING TECHNIQUE
Was *Anomalocaris* an apex predator, launching itself at shellfish and smashing them with its appendages? Some experts think so; others imagine that it hunted soft animals buried in the sediment, using its arms to grab them.

HOW DO YOU BRING BACK A WORLD THAT HAS DISAPPEARED?

BY GATHERING DIFFERENT FOSSILS FROM THE SAME PERIOD AND "GETTING THEM TALKING," A PALEONTOLOGIST CAN TRY TO IMAGINE ALL THE ANIMALS AND PLANTS OF AN ANCIENT LANDSCAPE. SO WHEN CHARLES WALCOTT DISCOVERED SOME STRANGE LITTLE FOSSILS IN THE BURGESS SHALE IN THE EARLY 1900S, HE THOUGHT THAT THE ANIMALS OF THE CAMBRIAN PERIOD WERE JELLYFISH AND ARTHROPOD ANCESTORS LIKE TRILOBITES.

IN THE 1970S, A TEAM OF RESEARCHERS RE-EXAMINED ALL THE FOSSILS AND CAME UP WITH A NEW PICTURE OF THIS VANISHED ECOSYSTEM. IN THIS RECONSTRUCTION, SLUGS COVERED IN PROTECTIVE SPINES AND SCALES (**WIWAXIA**) AND CURIOUS WORMS ON SPINES (**HALLUCIGENIA**) MOVE AROUND STATIONARY, WATER-FILTERING ORGANISMS (**DINOMISCHUS**). BURROWING WORMS STIR UP THE BOTTOM, WHILE OVERHEAD SWIMMERS SUCH AS **ANOMALOCARIS** ROAM THE WATERS.

SINCE THEN, OUR GUESSES ABOUT THIS 500-MILLION-YEAR-OLD LANDSCAPE HAVE CONTINUED TO CHANGE. NEW ANIMALS HAVE BEEN ADDED, SUCH AS **OTTOIA**, A PROBOSCID WORM DIGGING TUNNELS. ALSO, THE APPEARANCE OF ANIMALS LIKE **HALLUCIGENIA** OR **NECTOCARIS** HAS BEEN CORRECTED. SEVERAL STRANGE ATTRIBUTES OF THESE CREATURES ARE TODAY THOUGHT TO BE WEAPONS OF ATTACK (**OPABINIA**'S PROBOSCIS, **ANOMALOCARIS**'S ARTICULATED APPENDAGES) AND DEFENCE (**WIWAXIA**'S SPINES).

LIVING CREATURES AMONG THE PLANTS AND ANIMALS OF BURGESS: **(1)** JELLYFISH; **(2) CANADASPIS** (CRUSTACEAN); **(3) WAPTIA** (ARTHROPOD); **(4) SIDNEYIA** (ARTHROPOD); **(5) MARRELLA SPLENDENS** (TRILOBITE); **(6) VAUXIA**; **(7) DINOMISCHUS**; **(8) HALLUCIGENIA**; **(9) ANOMALOCARIS**; **(10) OPABINIA**; **(11) WIWAXIA** (MOLLUSC); **(12) NECTOCARIS** (POSSIBLE MOLLUSC); **(13) OTTOIA**; **(14) SANCTACARIS** (ARTHROPOD).

HALLUCIGENIA
THE CREATURE WITHOUT HEAD OR TAIL

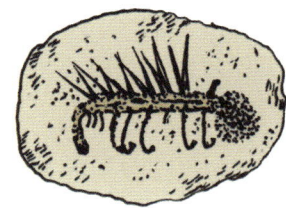

The small sea worm *Hallucigenia* is one of the strangest animals among the fossils found in the Burgess mountains. Paleontologists have made all kinds of guesses about how it looked and moved. They couldn't figure out which parts were its head or tail. They also weren't sure which parts were the top or the bottom! In the 1970s, they thought maybe it walked on pairs of spines and had a back covered in tentacles. This sci-fi reconstruction was literally reversed in the 1990s, when most agreed that the tentacles were the legs and the spines were on *Hallucigenia*'s back. Soon after this, the study of new fossils changed paleontologists' ideas again as they decided *Hallucigenia* had a different head than they'd previously thought.

- Found in Burgess, Canada (1909, renamed *Hallucigenia* in 1977)
- 10 to 50 mm long
- Lived 522 to 505 million years ago

A FACE REVEALED
Thanks to very detailed observation of *Hallucigenia* under an electron microscope, scientists have identified an elongated head, two eyes and a mouth lined with small spines.

IT'S ENOUGH TO MAKE YOU LOSE YOUR HEAD
Until very recently, the reconstructions of *Hallucigenia* had a bulbous head. But it seems that what scientists thought was the animal's head was actually a stain made by waste escaping from its anus. The head, then, would be at the other end.

WHAT IS THE REAL POWER OF "SNAKE STONES"?

STORM STONES
ONCE UPON A TIME, PEOPLE CALLED THESE "LIGHTNING STONES" AND SAID THEY FELL FROM THE SKY DURING THUNDERSTORMS. THEY ARE ACTUALLY THE FOSSILS OF BELEMNITES, ANIMALS NOT UNLIKE MODERN SQUID.

TONGUE STONES
FEELING SICK? MAYBE A "TONGUE STONE" COULD HELP! THAT'S WHAT MANY PEOPLE THOUGHT A LONG TIME AGO. "TONGUE STONES" ARE ACTUALLY FOSSILIZED SHARKS' TEETH—STILL HIGHLY VALUED BY FOSSIL-LOVERS TODAY!

AMULETS
IN SOME PARTS OF THE WORLD, TRILOBITE FOSSILS ARE WORN AS AMULETS, CARRIED EVERYWHERE FOR PROTECTION.

FAIRY LOAVES
IN ENGLAND, FOSSILIZED SEA URCHINS WERE CALLED "FAIRY LOAVES." SOME THOUGHT KEEPING THEM IN YOUR HOUSE MEANT YOU WOULD NEVER BE SHORT OF BREAD.

SNAKE STONES
ACCORDING TO AN ENGLISH LEGEND, SAINT HILDA WANTED TO BUILD A CONVENT IN A CERTAIN SPOT BUT IT WAS INFESTED WITH SNAKES…

SO SHE CHANGED THE SNAKES INTO ROCKS. REMEMBERING THIS LEGEND, FOR CENTURIES PEOPLE TOOK AMMONITE FOSSILS AND CARVED SNAKE HEADS ON THEM AND SOLD THEM AS MAGICAL OBJECTS.

THE STRANGE APPEARANCE OF FOSSILS HAS ALWAYS FASCINATED HUMANKIND. FOR CENTURIES, PEOPLE BELIEVED FOSSILS HAD MAGICAL AND HEALING POWERS AND CAME FROM STRANGE PLACES. THESE BELIEFS MADE THEM TALISMANS OR PRECIOUS COLLECTIBLES. SOMETIMES FOSSILS WERE EXHIBITED IN CABINETS OF CURIOSITIES. PROGRESS MADE BY SCIENCE IN THE 18TH AND 19TH CENTURIES GRADUALLY LED TO FOSSILS BEING SEEN FOR WHAT THEY ARE, THE REMAINS OF LIVING CREATURES THAT HAVE SINCE DISAPPEARED. EVEN SO, ISN'T IT MAGICAL TO HOLD IN YOUR HAND THE REMAINS OF A CREATURE THAT LIVED MILLIONS OF YEARS AGO?

AMMONOIDEA
COLLECTORS' FOSSILS

These fossils that look like coiled snakes have been known since ancient times because they are found in so many places. And now, of course, they are also found in the collections of nearly every fossil enthusiast!

Fossils of **Ammonoidea**, or ammonites, are plentiful, because they lived in the oceans for hundreds of millions of years. Paleontologists use them as chronological markers to date geological layers.

Ammonites were once shells that housed sea animals belonging to the class Cephalopoda. Today, the best known cephalopods are nautiluses, octopuses and squid.

- Known since antiquity
- 1 cm to 2 m in diameter
- Lived 408 to 66 million years ago

THE SUBMARINE OF ANCIENT TIMES
The ammonite's shell not only protected it but also helped it move. The animal could fill the spaces inside its shell with water to dive deeper or with gas to rise toward the surface.

DECORATION RESTORED
A few ammonite fossils still have traces of patterns on their shells. Comparing these with the shells of living aquatic animals, paleontologists assume that ammonites must have been decorated too.

HOW DID FISH LEARN TO WALK?

FOR MILLIONS OF YEARS, LIVING CREATURES WERE ALL AQUATIC. AT WHAT POINT, AND HOW, DID SOME ANIMALS LEAVE THE WATER? EXAMINING FOSSILS FROM MORE THAN 375 MILLION YEARS AGO, PALEONTOLOGISTS HAVE NOTICED THAT CERTAIN BONY FISH USED THEIR FINS TO DRAG THEMSELVES ALONG THE BOTTOM OF SHALLOW WATERS.

ONE OF THE FIRST VERTEBRATES (ANIMALS WITH A BACKBONE) PHYSICALLY CAPABLE OF LEAVING THE WATER WAS **TIKTAALIK**, A LARGE ANIMAL WITH FLESHY FINS. IT ALREADY HAD WRIST-LIKE JOINTS AND BONES THAT IN LATER ANIMALS WOULD EVOLVE INTO FINGERS AND TOES.

A FEW MILLION YEARS LATER, TWO PRIMITIVE AMPHIBIANS APPEARED THAT WERE BETTER ADAPTED TO WALKING. **ACANTHOSTEGA** HAD JOINTED LIMBS, EACH ENDING IN EIGHT WEBBED DIGITS, WHICH ALLOWED IT TO ROAM ACROSS THE BOTTOM OF THE MUDDY WATERS. MEANWHILE **ICHTHYOSTEGA** USED ITS TWO FRONT LEGS TO HAUL ITSELF FROM THE WATER AND DRAG ITSELF ALONG LIKE A SEAL.

LATER ON, **PEDERPES FINNEYAE** MIGHT HAVE BEEN THE FIRST AMPHIBIAN TO MOVE AROUND EASILY ON DRY LAND THANKS TO LEGS THAT ENDED IN FIVE DIGITS. THESE FIRST FOUR-LEGGED CREATURES TO VENTURE OUT OF THE WATER ARE THE ANCESTORS OF ALL LAND VERTEBRATES, FROM DINOSAURS TO HUMANS.

TIKTAALIK
THE WALKING FISH

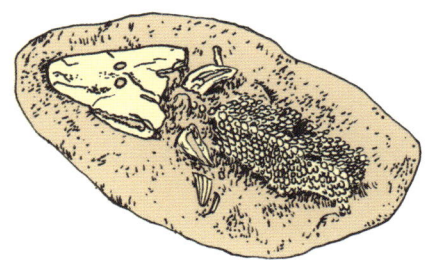

In 2004, an expedition to the Canadian Arctic discovered the fossilized remains of a creature dating back 375 million years. This animal shares features with the bony fish of its era, like gills and scales.

But scientists also noticed differences. They realized that the bones in its fins have joints that look like leg joints. The flattened shape of the skull and the position of the eye sockets are also unusual. These different clues led scientists to say that *Tiktaalik* might represent one stage in the evolution of fish towards amphibians, and therefore it might be one of the earliest ancestors of land vertebrates.

- Found in the Canadian Arctic (2004)
- 1.2 m to 2.7 m long
- Lived 384 to 376 million years ago

HIDDEN HANDS
Tiktaalik's fins, which look like those of a fish, not only could bend like legs but also had bones that look like toe bones.

A CHANGE OF SCENERY
Why did *Tiktaalik* venture onto the land? Was it searching for food, such as insects, or an environment free from predators where it could rest and lay its eggs?

REIGN OF THE REPTILES

The Mesozoic is the era of the dinosaurs and their reptile cousins in the air and the seas. This geological era, which stretched from 252 to 66 million years ago, began and ended with two great mass extinctions. It is divided into three periods: the Triassic, the Jurassic and the Cretaceous. The fossils of large reptiles like *Plesiosaurus* or *Mosasaurus* have excited scientists and non-scientists alike. As paleontologists have discovered many fossil-rich sites around the world, such as those in Mongolia's Gobi Desert, they have gradually reconstructed the animals of the Mesozoic.

These reconstructions have kept changing alongside new scientific discoveries. At first the animals were represented as dragons, then we imagined them as feathered dinosaurs, like **Archaeopteryx** and **Microraptor**. Scientists' ideas about these animals changed many times as more fossils were found or re-examined. We hear about these new discoveries and hypotheses from scientists but also see them explored in fictional books and movies. The first pictures of **Iguanodon** and **Diplodocus** launched "dinomania" at the start of the 20th century. Today **Tyrannosaurus** has become the icon of these vanished worlds.

HOW WAS THE MYSTERY OF THE THURINGIA FOOTPRINTS SOLVED?

IN 1833, STRANGE FOSSILIZED FOOTPRINTS WITH FIVE DIGITS, ONE OF WHICH RESEMBLED A THUMB, WERE FOUND IN THE THURINGIA REGION OF GERMANY.

IN A PERIOD WHEN KNOWLEDGE OF ANCIENT TIMES WAS VERY LIMITED, THE DISCOVERY OF THESE MYSTERIOUS FOOTPRINTS MADE PEOPLE WONDER. WAS IT A BEAR OR AN APE? OR EVEN A FISHERMAN WHO DIED IN THE FLOOD DESCRIBED IN THE BIBLE?

A FEW YEARS LATER, IN 1842, THE BRITISH SCIENTIST RICHARD OWEN, INSPIRED BY A TOOTH FRAGMENT UNCOVERED IN A SIMILAR GEOLOGICAL LAYER, THOUGHT HE HAD FOUND THE ANSWER. HE SAID THE FOOTPRINTS CAME FROM A GIANT AMPHIBIAN WITH A CROCODILE HEAD.

HOWEVER, SOMETHING ELSE INTRIGUED THE EXPERTS: THE FOSSILIZED FOOTPRINTS LOOKED WRONG, WITH THE THUMBS ON THE OUTSIDE, AS IF THE ANIMAL'S FEET HAD BEEN CROSSED OVER.

EARLY IN THE 20TH CENTURY, A GERMAN PALEONTOLOGIST OFFERED THE BEGINNINGS OF A SOLUTION. HE SAID THAT WHAT EVERYONE THOUGHT WAS A THUMB WAS ACTUALLY AN OUTER DIGIT.

ACCORDING TO HIM, THESE PRINTS BELONGED TO A PRIMITIVE REPTILE. BUT IT TOOK ANOTHER 40 YEARS, AND THE DISCOVERY OF FOSSILIZED BONES, BEFORE THE MYSTERY OF THE THURINGIA FOOTPRINTS WAS FINALLY SOLVED.

TICINOSUCHUS
A REPTILE UNMASKED

In the 1960s, French paleontologist Bernard Krebs discovered the fossil of a reptile dating from the Triassic period, in Ticino, Switzerland. He reconstructed the creature to resemble a crocodile but with a different leg structure. These legs also ended in five digits, one of which spread outwards.

It didn't take long to cross-check: the arrangement of the digits and the proportions of the legs in Krebs' reconstruction corresponded exactly to the Thuringia footprints, the mysterious trace fossils found in Germany in the 1830s. It had taken more than 130 years for the maker of those enigmatic tracks to be unmasked.

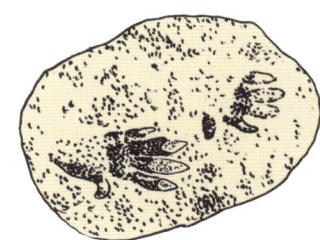

- Found in Switzerland (1965)
- 3 m long
- Lived 247 to 242 million years ago

ON THE TRAIL OF *TICINOSUCHUS*
Paleoichnology is the study of the preserved traces of extinct animals, and particularly their fossilized footprints. Series of footprints, known as trace fossils, provide precious information about the habits of long-vanished species. Putting together the *Ticinosuchus* skeleton with its footprints has made it possible to reconstruct how it walked.

A CROCODILE SKIN
The discovery of small fossilized plates around the skeleton of *Ticinosuchus* suggests that it had scaly skin like a crocodile, its very distant descendant.

HOW DID MARY ANNING BECOME A FAMOUS FOSSIL-HUNTER?

PLESIOSAURUS
THE PEACEABLE DRAGON OF THE SEA

The first reconstructions of *Plesiosaurus*, which showed it as a hybrid sea monster with a turtle's fins and snakelike neck, inspired many people. Fantastical novels and adventure stories like those by Jules Verne showed it swimming on the surface of the water, head raised, and often grappling with other creatures from these forgotten worlds (see p.40).

But later discoveries changed how scientists think it might have looked and behaved. Far from the picture of a terrifying sea dragon, today's paleontologists describe it as a large marine lizard, slow-moving, hunting only small prey and unable to lift its head from the water.

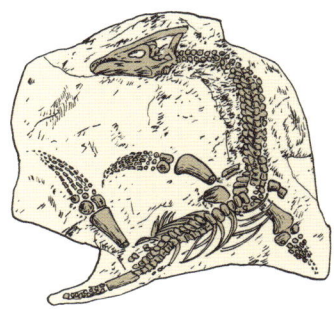

- Found in the United Kingdom (1821)
- 3 to 5 m long
- Lived 200 to 176 million years ago

HOW *PLESIOSAURUS* SWAM
How *Plesiosaurus* swam has long been a mystery. Scientists have recently tested a number of models to reconstruct its "underwater flight." The animal would have propelled itself with its two front fins and maintained stability with its rear ones.

THE REPTILE THAT DIDN'T LAY EGGS
Scientists thought for a long time that *Plesiosaurus* left the water to lay its eggs on dry land. But the recent discovery of a fossilized embryo inside a female's belly showed that *Plesiosaurus* gave birth to live young.

DID CHICKENS ONCE HAVE TEETH?

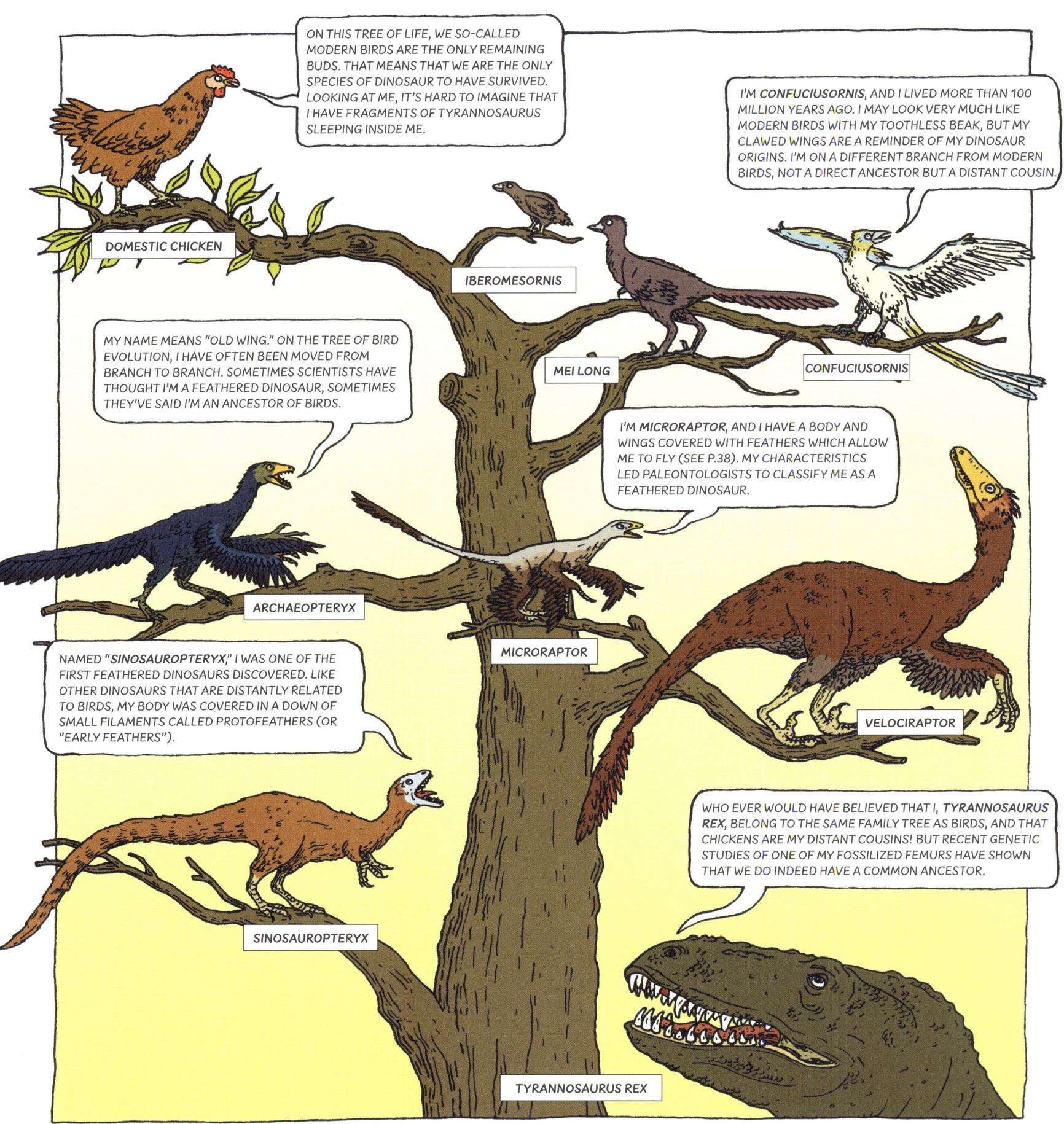

THE TREE OF LIFE ALLOWED DARWIN TO ILLUSTRATE HIS THEORY OF EVOLUTION. THE BUDS AT THE TEED OF THIS LARGE TREE'S BRANCHES REPRESENT CURRENT SPECIES, AND THE OLDEST BOUGHS LEADING TO THE NARROWER BRANCHES REPRESENT SPECIES THAT ARE EXTINCT, SOME OF WHICH ARE THE ANCESTORS OF TODAY'S SPECIES. SINCE THE DISCOVERY OF **ARCHAEOPTERYX** IN THE MIDDLE OF THE 19TH CENTURY, SCIENTISTS HAVE BEEN TRYING TO FIGURE OUT THE EVOLUTIONARY TREE CONNECTING BIRDS TO DINOSAURS. THIS TREE IS CONSTANTLY BEING REDRAWN AS NEW ANIMALS ARE ADDED, DISTANT COUSINS TO THE BIRDS WE SEE TODAY.

ARCHAEOPTERYX
THE OLDEST BIRD

Today paleontologists agree that dinosaurs have not completely disappeared: birds are their descendants. But it took a long time to see this connection. Scientists first began to wonder whether birds had evolved from dinosaurs when the fossil of *Archaeopteryx* was discovered in the 1860s. Finally John Ostrom's theories in the 1970s and then the discovery of feathered dinosaur fossils in the 1990s proved the link between birds and dinosaurs.

Nowadays, *Archaeopteryx* has become a symbol for Charles Darwin's theory of evolution (p.67) because it shows so clearly the step in between dinosaurs and birds.

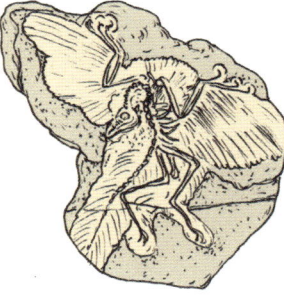

- Found in Germany (1861)
- 50 to 60 cm long
- Lived 152 to 145 million years ago

A NEW PLUMAGE
What did the feathers of a creature that disappeared millions of years ago look like? A scientist was recently able to examine the remains of pigments in fossilized feathers thanks to a powerful electron microscope. He deduced that *Archaeopteryx*'s plumage must have been black. But the feathers might have had other pigments too that have not been preserved.

FLIGHT
The question of *Archaeopteryx*'s flight is still widely debated. Did it climb a tree and then glide through the air? Or did it make short flights close to the ground the way chickens do?

HOW DID *DIPLODOCUS* BECOME A CELEBRITY?

IN 1898, THE ALMOST COMPLETE SKELETON OF A GIGANTIC CREATURE WAS UNEARTHED IN WYOMING BY AN EXPEDITION FINANCED BY BILLIONAIRE ANDREW CARNEGIE.

THE BONES WERE TAKEN TO THE PITTSBURGH MUSEUM. THERE SCIENTISTS BEGAN TO TRY TO RECONSTRUCT "THE MOST COLOSSAL CREATURE EVER TO WALK THE EARTH," ACCORDING TO THE NEWSPAPERS OF THE DAY. THE SPECIMEN WAS NAMED *DIPLODOCUS CARNEGII*, IN TRIBUTE TO CARNEGIE.

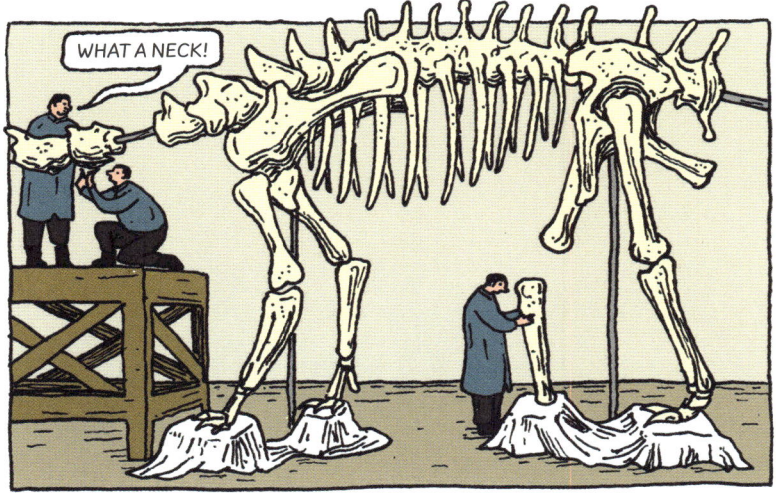

THE FOSSILIZED SKELETON'S FAME QUICKLY SPREAD BEYOND THE UNITED STATES. CONSIDERING THIS SUCCESS, IT WAS DECIDED TO MAKE COPIES OF EACH FOSSILIZED BONE OUT OF PLASTER SO PEOPLE IN MANY PLACES COULD SEE A LIFE SIZE *DIPLODOCUS* SKELETON.

THE PLASTER COPIES WERE SENT TO NATURAL HISTORY MUSEUMS IN LONDON, BERLIN, VIENNA, ST. PETERSBURG AND MEXICO.

IN 1908, THE NATURAL HISTORY MUSEUM IN PARIS RECEIVED ALMOST 300 PLASTER BONES, CAREFULLY PACKED IN CASES. AFTER IT WAS PATIENTLY PUT TOGETHER PARISIANS COULD FINALLY MARVEL AT THE FAMOUS *DIPLODOCUS* SKELETON.

OVER A FEW DECADES, INTERNATIONAL EXHIBITIONS OF *DIPLODOCUS* MADE THE ANIMAL A TRUE CELEBRITY. TO THIS DAY, THE SKELETON DOMINATES THE PALEONTOLOGY GALLERY OF PARIS'S BOTANICAL GARDENS.

DIPLODOCUS
THE NIMBLE COLOSSUS

Although the Pittsburgh fossil skeleton looked like a heavy, lumbering animal, *Diplodocus* is today described as a long, slender dinosaur with a lightweight skeleton. Its tail did not drag on the ground but was held horizontal and could be used to threaten attackers. Despite its enormous weight (twice that of an African elephant, the heaviest land animal alive today), *Diplodocus* could—in extreme situations like predator attack—stand on its hind legs. In addition, while *Diplodocus* was once drawn with its neck raised like a giraffe's, new studies show that the neck was not very flexible and could hardly be raised at all. Scientists also now think that this giant's back and tail were equipped with hard spines.

- Found in the United States of America (1877)
- 30 m long
- Lived 155 to 148 million years ago

A WHIP TAIL
The many long, thin vertebrae making up the tail of *Diplodocus* suggest that it was very flexible and used as a whip to defend itself.

THE LARGEST OF ALL THE DINOSAURS
When *Diplodocus* was discovered, scientists thought it was the largest animal ever to have lived. But it later lost this title to other animals in its group, the sauropods, such as *Brachiosaurus* in 1903, *Supersaurus* in 1985 and *Argentinosaurus* in 1993, which was over 40 m long. Will an even bigger dinosaur be discovered in the future?

WHO WON THE BONE WARS?

COMO BLUFF IS A ROCKY AREA IN WHAT TODAY IS WYOMING, USA. THE SITE IS FAMOUS FOR ITS POPULARITY WITH 19TH CENTURY PALEONTOLOGISTS IN SEARCH OF DINOSAUR BONES. OTHNIEL CHARLES MARSH WAS THE FIRST TO EXPLORE THESE RIDGES WHERE VAST FOSSILIZED BONES LAY EXPOSED ON THE GROUND.

COMO BLUFF PROVED TO BE A GOLDMINE FOR BONES. VERY SOON THE PALEONTOLOGISTS DISCOVERED AMAZING, PREVIOUSLY UNKNOWN SPECIMENS, SUCH AS ALLOSAURUS, APATOSAURUS AND EVEN THE NOW-FAMOUS **STEGOSAURUS**. HUNDREDS OF BONES WERE EXCAVATED, PACKED IN PLASTER AND PLACED INTO LARGE WOODEN CRATES. PRETTY SOON, THE PALEONTOLOGIST EDWARD COPE, MARSH'S ARCH-RIVAL, HEARD ABOUT IT, TOO.

A MAD RACE FOR DISCOVERY BEGAN: A RUSH FOR BONES THAT TURNED INTO OPEN WARFARE. BOTH SIDES SPIED ON, SABOTAGED, AND EVEN DESTROYED THEIR OPPONENTS' DISCOVERIES. PALEONTOLOGY BECAME A COMBAT SPORT WHERE NO ONE HESITATED TO THROW PUNCHES IN ORDER TO CLAIM OR PROTECT THEIR DISCOVERIES. THESE BONE WARS, DESPITE THEIR NASTINESS, LED TO IMPORTANT DISCOVERIES AND HELPED MAKE PALEONTOLOGY POPULAR.

STEGOSAURUS
THE SPINY GIANT OF THE JURASSIC

Stegosaurus was one of the famous dinosaurs discovered by Othniel Charles Marsh during the bone wars. The paleontologists were curious about strange fossilized plates they found close to its spine. At first they thought the plates lay flat on *Stegosaurus*'s back (hence the name, which means "roofed reptile"). Then it was decided that they instead stood up vertically like large spikes. Study of the cranium showed that the animal's brain was small compared to its large size. This small brain led some to think it was stupid, an idea then applied to all dinosaurs. Though people once saw it as slow, today's scientists believe that *Stegosaurus* could be agile in certain circumstances.

- Found in the United States of America (1877)
- 9 m long
- Lived 155 to 148 million years ago

COMBATA-SAURUS
Several clues show that this peaceful herbivore could become a fierce fighter against big carnivores. In defence, it would rotate its body to strike powerful blows with its spiked tail, seriously wounding its enemies.

IDENTITY PLATES
For some time, *Stegosaurus*'s plates were seen as weapons of defence or as a temperature-regulating mechanism. Today we describe them instead as a way to impress enemies and attract mates.

HOW DID "DINOMANIA" BEGIN?

IN 1851, THE VAST GLASS AND IRON "CRYSTAL PALACE" WAS BUILT IN LONDON TO HOST THE FIRST WORLD'S FAIR. AFTER THE EVENT, THE BUILDING WAS MOVED TO SOUTH LONDON, AND THE ARTIST BENJAMIN WATERHOUSE HAWKINS WAS ASKED TO BUILD LIFE-SIZED SCULPTURES OF ANIMALS FROM ANCIENT TIMES TO LIVEN UP THE SURROUNDING PARK. OF ALL THE CREATURES, WHICH ONES GOT THE MOST ATTENTION? DINOSAURS!

TO CREATE THE DINOSAUR SCULPTURES, HAWKINS FOLLOWED THE SCIENTIFIC ADVICE OF PALEONTOLOGIST SIR RICHARD OWEN. OWEN HAD GIVEN THE NAME "DINOSAUR" TO THE GIGANTIC CREATURES WHOSE FOSSILIZED REMAINS HAD RECENTLY BEEN UNEARTHED. *MEGALOSAURUS*, ***IGUANODON*** AND *HYLAEOSAURUS* WERE BROUGHT TOGETHER IN THE FAMILY OF "FEARSOMELY LARGE LIZARDS," AKA "DINOSAURS."

PEOPLE IN BRITAIN WERE VERY EXCITED ABOUT THIS AMUSEMENT PARK SHOWING THESE NEWLY DISCOVERED CREATURES. IN 1853, AS A SPECTACULAR PUBLICITY STUNT TO CELEBRATE THE NEW YEAR, A TABLE WAS SET UP INSIDE AN ***IGUANODON*** SCULPTURE. MANY PEOPLE READ ABOUT IT IN THE NEWS. LITTLE DID THEY KNOW THIS WOULD UNLEASH "DINOMANIA."

IGUANODON
THE DINOSAUR WITH "A THOUSAND FACES"

The way we picture *Iguanodon* today is very different from Benjamin Waterhouse Hawkins's sculpture. He made it look like a fat rhinoceros with a horn on its nose. Then scientists discovered a large fossil deposit in Belgium at the end of the 19th century and thought maybe *Iguanodon* looked like a giant kangaroo, up on its hind legs and leaning on a big muscular tail. The latest studies show that it was both bipedal and quadrupedal: *Iguanodon* would usually have moved on all fours but could rear up on its hind legs to reach vegetation or to defend itself against predators.

- Found in England (1809)
- Up to 10 m long
- Lived 139 to 100 million years ago

A BEAKED HERBIVORE
Iguanodon's jawbone tells us what it ate. Though it was a powerful creature, it was not a carnivore. Its horned beak and flattened teeth helped it cut and chew vegetation.

AN ALL-IN-ONE HAND
Studying *Iguanodon*'s fossilized hand has shown that it had several functions: the animal used its three middle fingers for walking and its "little finger" for grabbing hold of plants.

A DAGGER THUMB
The hand ended in a clawed thumb, which was probably used for stabbing predators. When this claw was first found, scientists thought it belonged on the animal's nose as a horn.

HOW DID THE ANCESTORS OF BIRDS LEARN TO FLY?

PEOPLE HAVE BEEN WONDERING SINCE THE EARLY 20TH CENTURY HOW FEATHERED DINOSAURS LEFT THE GROUND TO BECOME FLYING ANIMALS. PALEONTOLOGISTS THEN BELIEVED—BASED ON THE SMALL NUMBER OF FOSSILS AVAILABLE—THAT THESE ANIMALS COULD CLIMB INTO TREES TO LIVE THERE. LEGS COVERED IN FEATHERS WOULD HAVE ALLOWED THEM TO GLIDE DOWN, BREAKING THE SPEED OF THEIR FALL LIKE A PARACHUTE.

OTHER SCIENTISTS THOUGHT OF THESE FAMOUS BIRD ANCESTORS AS RUNNING BIPEDS, BEATING HARD WITH THEIR FEATHERED FRONT LIMBS, AND TAKING OFF FROM THE GROUND. THEY THOUGHT THAT THE FIRST FLIGHT WOULD HAVE BEEN BY FLAPPING RATHER THAN GLIDING. THE SMALL NUMBER OF KNOWN FOSSILS AT THE TIME COULDN'T PROVE EITHER IDEA.

THE DISCOVERIES OF FEATHERED DINOSAUR FOSSILS IN CHINA IN THE 1990S AND 2000S GAVE MORE INFORMATION. THE STUDY OF DINOSAURS WITH FOUR WINGS LIKE *MICRORAPTOR* SEEMS TO CONFIRM THAT SOME SPECIES LEARNED TO FLY BY GLIDING, WHILE OTHER SPECIES WERE GLIDING AND FLAPPING AT THE SAME TIME.

MICRORAPTOR
THE FOUR-WINGED DINOSAUR

In 2003, an astonishing discovery was made in China of a curious little dinosaur with feathers on both front and rear limbs. Was this creature able to fly and, if so, how? Knowing that *Microraptor* lived in trees and could climb them easily thanks to its large hooked claws, scientists have tried to reconstruct its aerial movement using models. While it seems likely that it launched itself and glided from one tree to another, we're still not sure what it looked like while it was flying or whether it flapped its wings.

- Found in China (2003)
- 70 cm long
- Lived 130 to 126 million years ago

A SMALL DINOSAUR
The best-known dinosaurs tend to be the largest. Yet dinosaur species existed in all sizes, including very small ones like *Microraptor*.

A NOCTURNAL HUNTER
The rings of bone around its eyes resemble those of today's nocturnal birds, suggesting that it hunted at night.

DID DINOSAURS HAVE SCALES, FUR OR FEATHERS?

SINCE THE FIRST FOSSILS WERE IDENTIFIED IN THE MID 19TH CENTURY, PEOPLE HAVE ASKED WHAT THESE CREATURES NAMED "DINOSAURS" ACTUALLY LOOKED LIKE. WITH ONLY RANDOM BONES AND A FEW INCOMPLETE SKELETONS, PALEONTOLOGISTS USED THEIR IMAGINATIONS TO RECONSTRUCT THESE "FEARSOMELY LARGE LIZARDS." THEIR FIRST DESCRIPTIONS WERE OF MYTHICAL DRAGONS AND TERRIFYING SEA MONSTERS.

AS PALEONTOLOGY PROGRESSED, THE RECONSTRUCTIONS GOT MORE PRECISE. PALEONTOLOGISTS COULD IMAGINE DINOSAUR SHAPES, MOVEMENTS AND ABILITIES BY COMPARING DINOSAURS WITH REPTILES TODAY. THE PAINTINGS OF CHARLES ROBERT KNIGHT AT THE START OF THE 20TH CENTURY USUALLY SHOWED THEM AS HUGE AND HEAVY, WITH THICK SKIN IN GREENS OR GREYS, LUMBERING SLOWLY ABOUT.

NEW DISCOVERIES SUCH AS **DEINONYCHUS** CHANGED THE PICTURE AGAIN THROUGH THE 1970s. THE HEAVY, COLD-BLOODED LUMPS SCIENTISTS HAD IMAGINED BEFORE WERE REPLACED BY A VISION OF ACTIVE ANIMALS, WITH OBVIOUS MUSCLES AND MORE VIVID AND PATTERNED SKIN. SCIENTISTS BEGAN TO QUESTION HOW MUCH DINOSAURS WERE LIKE MODERN REPTILES OR WHETHER THEY WERE MORE LIKE MAMMALS AND BIRDS.

IN THE 1990S, SEVERAL DISCOVERIES IN CHINA OF SMALL FEATHERED DINOSAURS MATCHED SCIENTISTS' GUESSES BASED ON EVIDENCE OF FEATHERS IN OTHER FOSSILS. A NEW REVOLUTION IN HOW WE SAW DINOSAURS BEGAN: ANIMALS LIKE **DEINONYCHUS** AND **VELOCIRAPTOR** WERE NOW THOUGHT TO BE COVERED IN FEATHERS.

DEINONYCHUS
THE NEW DINOSAUR

By the time the American paleontologist John Ostrom discovered and described *Deinonychus* in the 1960s, scientists and the general public were showing less interest in dinosaurs. By presenting *Deinonychus* as a lively, agile predator, birdlike in its shape and movements, he went against the reptilian image of dinosaurs of the time. His description brought about a new craze for prehistoric times.

Ostrom also revived earlier hypotheses that birds evolved from dinosaurs. Recent discoveries of feathered dinosaurs in China (the *Microraptor*, p.39) have proved these hypotheses correct.

- Found in the United States of America (1964)
- 3 m long
- Lived 115 to 108 million years ago

A HELL OF A CLAWING
The sickle-shaped claws on *Deinonychus*'s hind legs appear to have been a formidable weapon. Scientists first thought they were used to slash prey or grasp large animals. Today scientists think they used their claws like raptors to pin their prey to the ground in order to eat it.

TERRIFYING TEAMWORK
Deinonychus is often shown hunting in packs. The discovery of several *Deinonychus* specimens surrounding the fossil of a large herbivore, *Tenontosaurus*, was considered proof of their cooperative hunting.

HOW DO YOU DRAW A DINOSAUR?

PROTOCERATOPS
THE HERBIVORE OF THE CRETACEOUS

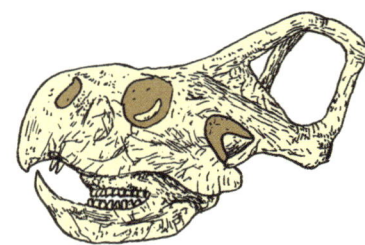

In 1922, an American expedition in Mongolia discovered the fossils of a small herbivore with a neck frill. **Protoceratops** is thought to have been widespread in the Gobi Desert during the Cretaceous period because so many of its fossils have been found since then. This abundance of specimens points towards gregarious behaviour.

Because scientists have found **Protoceratops** adult fossils gathered around nests and the fossils of youngsters, they believe that parents took care of their young, nursing them and bringing food to the nest.

- Found in Mongolia (1922)
- 2 m long
- Lived 84 to 72 million years ago

THE ORIGIN OF THE GRIFFIN MYTH?

What if the legend of the griffin, a hybrid creature resembling a winged lion, started when early gold miners found **Protoceratops** fossils in the Gobi Desert? This idea was proposed by Adrienne Mayor, an American historian specializing in myths and legends.

HOW WAS THE "EGG STEALER" ACQUITTED?

IN THE 1920S A SKELETON WAS DISCOVERED WITH A CRUSHED SKULL NEAR A NEST OF EGGS BELIEVED TO BE THOSE OF A **PROTOCERATOPS**. PALEONTOLOGISTS RECONSTRUCTED A CRIME SCENE: AN **OVIRAPTOR** ("EGG STEALER") DINOSAUR CAUGHT RED-HANDED AND ATTACKED BY A **PROTOCERATOPS** DEFENDING ITS NEST.

BUT 70 YEARS LATER, THE CASE WAS REOPENED. THANKS TO NEW EVIDENCE, **OVIRAPTOR** WAS DECLARED INNOCENT. THE STUDY OF AN EGG LIKE THOSE FOUND IN 1923 AND CONTAINING AN EMBRYO FOSSIL SHOWED THAT THE **OVIRAPTOR** IN THE FIRST DISCOVERY WAS NOT STEALING EGGS BUT RATHER TRYING TO PROTECT ITS OWN FROM A PREDATOR.

SOME YEARS LATER, THE DISCOVERY OF AN **OVIRAPTOR** SKELETON SQUATTING ON A NEST CHANGED THE REPTILE IMAGE OF THE ANIMAL SCIENTISTS HAD BEFORE. NOW THE PICTURE HAS DEVELOPED A LOT SINCE THE START OF THE 20TH CENTURY. TODAY'S EXPERTS SHOW **OVIRAPTOR** AS A DINOSAUR COVERED IN FEATHERS, SITTING ON ITS EGGS LIKE A BIRD.

OVIRAPTOR
THE MOTHER-HEN DINOSAUR

Scientists long believed that dinosaurs buried their eggs in the dirt and sand, as most reptiles do. The discovery in 1993 of a squatting *Oviraptor* fossil among fossilized eggs showed rather that it built nests on the ground and sat on its eggs. This not only cleared its name as an "egg stealer" but also strengthened the evidence that many dinosaur species could be compared to birds. And so, far from its early reptilian depictions, this dinosaur is shown today as a large, birdlike animal sitting on its eggs to keep them warm and safe.

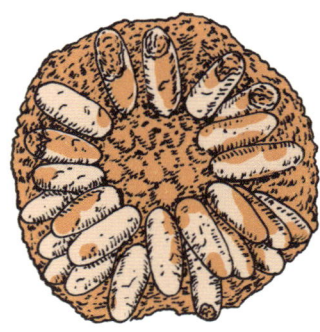

- Found in Mongolia (1923)
- 1.6 m long
- Lived 80 to 72 million years ago

A FEATHERED DINOSAUR
Even though it couldn't fly, *Oviraptor* had feathers. These must have had other uses: to attract mates, for warmth, or to shelter babies?

AN ORDERLY NEST
Paleontologists were surprised at *Oviraptor*'s fossilized brood, which were found arranged in a circle.

WHAT WAS *PARASAUROLOPHUS*'S CREST FOR?

WHEN PALEONTOLOGISTS IN THE EARLY 1900S DISCOVERED FOSSILS OF A DINOSAUR THAT THEY NAMED **PARASAUROLOPHUS**, THEY WERE IMPRESSED BY THE LONG RIDGE ON ITS HEAD.

THEY CAME UP WITH ALL KINDS OF IDEAS FOR THE RIDGE'S PURPOSE, INCLUDING THAT IT GAVE THE ANIMAL SPECIAL ABILITIES. ONE OF THE MOST SURPRISING SUGGESTIONS WAS THAT THIS CREST HID CHEMICAL GLANDS THAT ALLOWED THE ANIMAL TO SPIT A CORROSIVE, BOILING LIQUID.

PARASAUROLOPHUS WAS ALSO THOUGHT TO BE ABLE TO SWIM AND FEED UNDERWATER. ITS CREST, A LONG TUBE CONNECTED TO ITS NOSTRILS, COULD HAVE WORKED AS A SNORKEL, SOME SUGGESTED.

OTHER EXPERTS SAW THE CREST AS A POSSIBLE JOUSTING WEAPON. BUT TODAY MOST SCIENTISTS THINK IT WAS DECORATION THAT BECAME BRIGHT AND VIVID DURING THE MATING SEASON.

FINALLY, BECAUSE THE CREST WAS HOLLOW, SOME SCIENTISTS THINK IT WOULD HAVE MADE **PARASAUROLOPHUS**'S CALLS EVEN LOUDER.

IT'S FUN TO IMAGINE THESE LARGE ANIMALS "TRUMPETING" IN THE FORESTS OF THE CRETACEOUS, CALLING BACK AND FORTH, WARNING OTHERS OF DANGER, OR ASSERTING THEIR DOMINANCE.

PARASAUROLOPHUS
THE TENOR OF EXTINCT TIMES

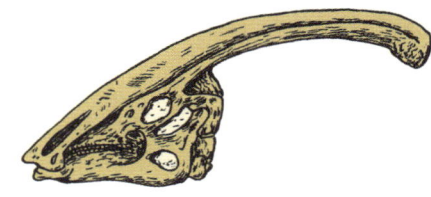

Parasaurolophus is a member of the hadrosaur family, which were nicknamed "the duck-billed dinosaurs" and believed for a time to be semi-aquatic. Several features, such as the duck-like beak and the muscular tail like a crocodile's, suggested an animal that moved about in water. Some even thought that it used its crest as a snorkel. Nowadays, judging from its jaws and teeth, paleontologists believe that it was a land herbivore. The role of its crest still raises questions. Was it to catch the eye of mates, a way to make loud sounds or for keeping their bodies at the right temperature?

- Found in Canada (1920)
- 9 m long
- Lived 76 to 74 million years ago

A VOICE SILENCED...
How do you recover the calls of a creature living millions of years ago? It seems impossible since the soft tissue used to produce sound in vertebrates is hardly ever fossilized.

...BUT MAYBE REDISCOVERED
Studying *Parasaurolophus*'s striking crest offers the beginnings of an answer. By pushing air through a tube of a similar shape, researchers produced a sound like that of a foghorn.

A NEW LOOK
The appearance of dinosaurs' skin is still a matter of debate. It seems likely that their skin was bright and vivid. Experts believe that during mating season, the crests of male *Parasaurolophus* really caught the eye.

HOW WAS THE MONSTER OF MAASTRICHT REVEALED?

HOW ASTONISHED THE WORKERS IN THE UNDERGROUND QUARRIES IN MAASTRICHT, THE NETHERLANDS, MUST HAVE BEEN IN 1766 WHEN THEY DISCOVERED A MONSTROUS FOSSILIZED SKULL!

THE WORKERS NOTIFIED DR. HOFFMAN, THE TOWN SURGEON AND LOCAL FOSSIL COLLECTOR. HE SAW THE IMPORTANCE OF THE FIND AND OVERSAW THE WORK TO DIG OUT THE SKULL.

AT A TIME WHEN DINOSAURS WERE STILL UNKNOWN, THE FOSSIL MADE PEOPLE THINK OF MORE FAMILIAR ANIMALS. THE DOCTOR THOUGHT IT WAS THE SKULL OF A GIGANTIC CROCODILE. OTHER SCHOLARS SAW IT AS THE REMAINS OF A WHALE.

IN 1794, FRENCH REVOLUTIONARY TROOPS ATTACKED THE TOWN OF MAASTRICHT AND TOOK THE MONSTER'S FOSSIL AS BOOTY. THE FOLLOWING YEAR, IT REACHED THE NATURAL HISTORY MUSEUM IN PARIS, WHERE IT WAS PUT ON DISPLAY.

IN PARIS, A VERY YOUNG SCIENTIST BY THE NAME OF GEORGES CUVIER BEGAN STUDYING THE FOSSIL. HIS METHOD WAS TO COMPARE IT TO CONTEMPORARY ANIMAL SKELETONS. HIS FINDINGS WERE NEW.

CUVIER SAID THE GREAT "MAASTRICHT ANIMAL" WAS SIMILAR TO THE MONITOR LIZARD AND LIVED IN THE SEA. BUT HE WENT EVEN FURTHER AND SAID THAT THE SPECIES NO LONGER EXISTED. THIS SEEMED TO CONFIRM A NEW IDEA THAT MANY SPECIES HAD BECOME EXTINCT IN THE PAST. A REVOLUTIONARY THOUGHT AT THE TIME...

MOSASAURUS
THE *T. REX* OF THE SEAS

After the skull was discovered in Maastricht, many other *Mosasaurus* fossils were found around the world. Nowadays, paleontologists know much more about this huge sea reptile. As Georges Cuvier quite correctly showed, mosasaurs are sea lizards, close relatives of today's species like monitor lizards. Many clues suggest that it was the apex predator of the seas in the Cretaceous period. Its sleek body of gigantic proportions, its huge flexible jaw that could open and close in the blink of an eye, and its sharp teeth would have enabled it to attack prey such as plesiosaurs. While *Tyrannosaurus rex* was carrying out its reign of terror on the Cretaceous land, *Mosasaurus* ruled the depths of the sea.

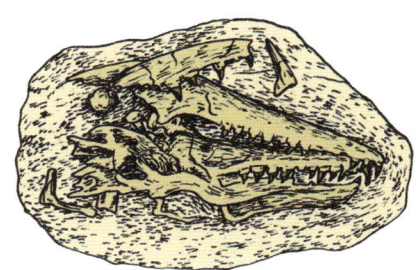

- Found in The Netherlands (1766)
- Up to 18 m long
- Lived 70 to 66 million years ago

...FOR NEW SWIMMING
After comparing this new tail with that of a shark, experts now think *Mosasaurus* could swim much faster than previously thought. It would have moved quickly thanks to a stiff body propelled like a torpedo by its powerful undulating tail.

A NEW TAIL...
Mosasaurus was pictured moving like an eel with a swaying body that ended in a flattened tail. After a closer look at a detailed fossil, scientists have recently come up with a new possible design for the shape of its tail.

HOW DID *T. REX* BECOME A MOVIE STAR?

ALREADY MADE FAMOUS BY THE AMERICAN PRESS AT THE START OF THE 20TH CENTURY, **TYRANNOSAURUS REX** FIRST APPEARED IN MOVIES IN 1925 IN *THE LOST WORLD*, THE FIRST MONSTER MOVIE. BUT IN THIS ADAPTATION OF THE NOVEL BY ARTHUR CONAN DOYLE, IT HAD ONLY A SUPPORTING ROLE ALONGSIDE MORE MEMORABLE DINOSAURS LIKE *TRICERATOPS*, *BRONTOSAURUS* AND EVEN *ALLOSAURUS*.

A FEW YEARS LATER, IN 1933, **T. REX** WAS BACK IN FRONT OF THE CAMERA IN THE MOVIE *KING KONG*, THE STORY OF AN EXPEDITION TO A MYSTERIOUS ISLAND INHABITED BY A GIANT APE AND DINOSAURS. IN A NOW-FAMOUS SCENE, THE "KING OF THE TERRIBLE LIZARDS" WAS PITTED IN COMBAT AGAINST THE MIGHTY KING KONG. **T. REX** WAS PORTRAYED AS A SORT OF DINO-KANGAROO, WITH A WALKING-JUMPING GAIT.

FOR MANY YEARS, **T. REX** PLAYED THE PART OF THE BIG BULLY. AFTER THE SECOND WORLD WAR, IT FEATURED IN MANY POOR-QUALITY MOVIES, WHERE IT LIVED ANACHRONISTICALLY ALONGSIDE PREHISTORIC HUMANS. IT WAS EVEN SEEN WALKING ON ITS HIND LEGS, BODY VERTICAL, TAIL DRAGGING ON THE GROUND, A REPRESENTATION THAT THE SCIENTIFIC WORLD ABANDONED IN THE 1960S.

WE HAD TO WAIT UNTIL THE 1990S, WITH STEPHEN SPIELBERG'S MOVIE *JURASSIC PARK*, FOR **T. REX** TO GET THE PART IT DESERVED. IN THIS STORY WHERE HUMANS BRING DINOSAURS BACK TO LIFE, **T. REX** GETS A MAKEOVER AND TURNS OUT TO HAVE SERIOUS SCREEN PRESENCE. BOTH VAST AND AGILE, IT GIVES A PERFECT PERFORMANCE AS THE TERRIFYING PREDATOR. RECOGNITION AT LAST: **T. REX** HAD BECOME THE STAR OF THE DINOSAURS.

TYRANNOSAURUS
THE ICON OF VANISHED WORLDS

Following the success of the movie *Jurassic Park*, **Tyrannosaurus rex** became the iconic dinosaur. Building on scientific discoveries of the 1970s (see p.40), *Jurassic Park* finally allowed **T. rex** to shed the kangaroo-dinosaur outfit it had been stuck with for so long.

But today scientists have changed their minds again. Although it is accepted that **T. rex** was indeed an apex predator with an uncommonly powerful jaw, *Jurassic Park* does seem to have exaggerated its running speed and the power of its roar.

- Found in the United States of America (1874)
- 12 m long
- Lived 68 to 66 million years ago

GOING OVER THE SPEED LIMIT
Study of the rare footprint impressions left by *T. rex* and its anatomy show that it could not have run faster than 29 km/ 18 mi. per hour, well below the speed we see in *Jurassic Park*.

A TERRIBLE GURGLING
Is it possible to reconstruct a dinosaur's roar? While some paleontologists think not yet, others have tried to simulate the sound of *T. rex*. A far cry from the roars in *Jurassic Park*, the sounds they got were closer to gurgles or crocodile grunts.

THE AGE OF MAMMALS AND BIRDS

The most recent era, the Cenozoic, began 66 million years ago and continues to this day. It started after the mass extinction known as the Cretaceous–Paleogene extinction event, which eliminated most animal species at the time. On land, all large animals died out; the survivors included small mammals like **Purgatorius**. This era is often referred to as the age of mammals, because most mammals evolved during this time. But many birds that descended from dinosaurs have also done well. Although it remains hard to reconstruct some species that have disappeared during the Cenozoic, their closeness to today's animals helps paleontologists in their work. Anatomical—and now also genetic—studies of fossils can lead scientists to more and more accurate descriptions of these creatures from the past. The family trees of today's animals have been enriched by the discovery of new ancestors like **Pakicetus**.

HOW DO YOU SURVIVE A MASS EXTINCTION?

GEOLOGICAL EVIDENCE SHOWS THAT SEVERAL TIMES EARTH HAS BEEN THE VICTIM OF HUGE UPHEAVALS THAT LED TO THE DISAPPEARANCE OF COUNTLESS ANIMAL SPECIES. SCIENTISTS EXAMINING THE ROCK STRATA HAVE IDENTIFIED FIVE MAJOR CRISES. THE LARGEST OF THE EXTINCTIONS HAPPENED MORE THAN 245 MILLION YEARS AGO AND LED TO MORE THAN 95% OF SPECIES BEING WIPED OUT. THE MOST RECENT BIG EVENT, KNOWN AS THE CRETACEOUS–PALEOGENE EXTINCTION EVENT, TOOK PLACE 66 MILLION YEARS AGO. IT SAW THE END OF THE LARGE DINOSAURS, BUT THINGS TURNED OUT WELL FOR ANIMALS LIKE MAMMALS AND BIRDS. THIS IS THE STORY OF ONE OF THOSE SURVIVORS.

PURGATORIUS
THE LITTLE SURVIVOR

While *Purgatorius* did not live alongside the dinosaurs, it belongs to the family of small mammals that managed miraculously to survive the catastrophe that led to the dinosaurs' extinction. For a long time, paleontologists only knew about a few of its teeth. From these, scientists thought *Purgatorius* ate insects, flowers and fruit. Comparing the fossils to the teeth of other mammals, scientists decided that *Purgatorius* looked like a small rodent with a pointy muzzle. Nevertheless, when paleontologists try to understand its connection to other mammals, they see *Purgatorius* as an ancestor of primates.

- Found in the United States of America (1965)
- 10 cm long
- Lived 66 to 63 million years ago

FROM THE GROUND TO THE TREES
At first, scientists thought that *Purgatorius* lived on the ground. But the recent discovery of a fossilized ankle bone changed their minds. Now they think it was arboreal, an animal that moved around in the trees.

TALKATIVE TEETH
Teeth are often the only thing left from mammals because they are made of such a hard material: enamel. Teeth tell us a lot—what an animal ate and where it lived.

WHAT FAMILY SECRET IS THE WHALE HIDING?

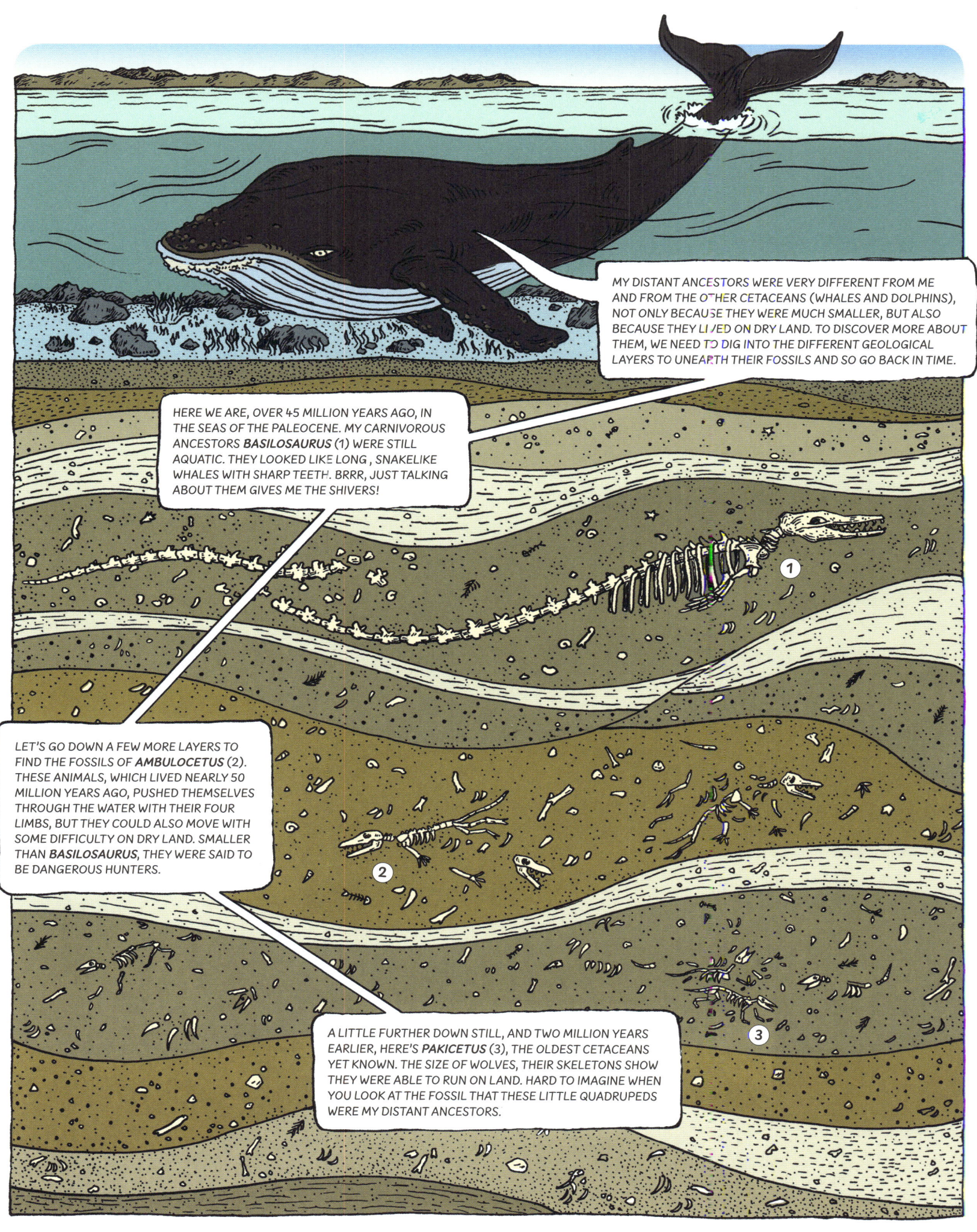

PAKICETUS
THE WHALE WITH LEGS

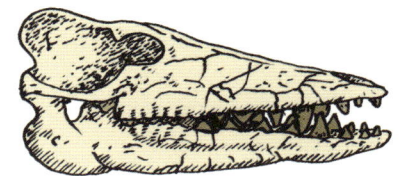

In the late 1970s, paleontologists unearthed the fossilized skull of a previously unknown animal, *Pakicetus*. A study of its ear revealed it to be a member of the Cetacea, the whales and dolphins, and a possible ancestor of today's whales. But imagine the paleontologists' surprise a few years later when they discovered a complete skeleton of the same animal, confirming that *Pakicetus* was a quadruped and likely to have lived on land rather than in the water. Its feet, ending in digits with small hooves, even meant it could run on land. Around 50 million years ago, this furry carnivore would have been found in and out of rivers, hunting fish and other small prey. Since we think all life began in the water, *Pakicetus*'s ancestors came out of the water to evolve into land animals. Then it seems that *Pakicetus*'s descendants gradually left the land to return to the water until they were once again totally aquatic, just like their very distant ancestors.

- Found in Pakistan (1981)
- 1–2 m long
- Lived 53 to 47 million years ago

PEERLESS EARS
Pakicetus's skull is that of an amphibious animal—that is, able to move in water and on land. Like the other cetaceans, its ear structure shows that it could detect and locate sounds under the water.

HOW WERE THE MESSEL FOSSILS PRESERVED?

MILLIONS OF YEARS AGO, IN EUROPE, THERE WAS A BIG LAKE BORDERED BY A TROPICAL FOREST. MANY ANIMALS LIVED IN THE HOT AND HUMID CLIMATE (1). BUT ONE DAY, A SUDDEN AND MYSTERIOUS CATASTROPHE KILLED SOME OF THE ANIMALS. THE EXACT CAUSE IS STILL DEBATED. WAS THE LAKE POISONED BY BACTERIA? DID THE AIR AND WATER BECOME TOXIC AFTER A VOLCANO IN THE LAKE RELEASED A DEADLY GAS (2)?

WHATEVER THE CAUSE, THE BODIES OF POISONED ANIMALS FELL TO THE BOTTOM OF THE LAKE (3). THE ALMOST STAGNANT WATER, WITH LITTLE OXYGEN, MEANT THE BODIES WERE WELL PRESERVED. COVERED BY LAYERS OF MUD, THEY WERE TRANSFORMED OVER TIME INTO MINERALS—THAT IS, INTO FOSSILS (4).

MILLIONS OF YEARS LATER, THE LAKE DISAPPEARED AND THE MESSEL SITE BECAME A TREASURE TROVE FOR PALEONTOLOGISTS. THE FOSSILIZED ANIMALS WERE REALLY WELL PRESERVED (5). THE STUDY OF THOUSANDS OF FOSSILS FROM THE SITE LED TO THE PRECISE RECONSTRUCTION OF A 50-MILLION-YEAR-OLD ECOSYSTEM.

PROPALAEOTHERIUM
THE MINIATURE HORSE

Although the first bones of *Propalaeotherium* were discovered in the middle of the 19th century, the unusually well-preserved fossils uncovered since the 1970s at the Messel site in Germany have given much more information about this animal and how it lived. Studies of skin impressions, the fossilized contents of its stomach and traces of its fur revealed a precise picture. It's hard to imagine that this small mammal that lived in dense forests is the distant ancestor of today's horses, which are adapted to vast plains. In between these two animals—separated by 45 million years—paleontologists have found many species, allowing them to reconstruct the horse's family tree and its evolution.

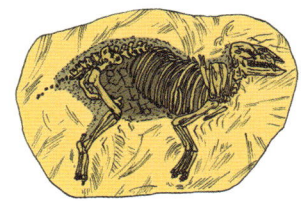

- Found in France (1849)
- 30 to 60 cm tall
- Lived 50 to 41 million years ago

A HORSE WITHOUT HOOVES
Propalaeotherium walked on the pads of its four-toed feet. Its descendants are today's horses, whose "toes" are now a single hoof. Horses' long legs evolved as an adaptation to running in more open terrain.

A MEAL FOR ALL ETERNITY
Thanks to a *Propalaeotherium*'s fossilized stomach contents, paleontologists found that the animal's last meal consisted of leaves and grapes.

WHAT FOSSIL TREASURES WERE FOUND IN THE GOBI DESERT?

EXTRACT FROM THE (PRETEND) LOG OF ROY CHAPMAN ANDREWS
JUNE 2, 1922
AFTER MANY DAYS ON THE ROAD, MY TEAM AND I HAVE FINALLY REACHED THE EDGE OF ONE OF THE MOST INHOSPITABLE AREAS ON EARTH— THE GOBI DESERT IN MONGOLIA. THE AMERICAN MUSEUM OF NATURAL HISTORY HAS SENT US TO BRING BACK THE FOSSILS OF EARLY HUMANS. THE EXPEDITION PROMISES TO BE PERILOUS.

NOVEMBER 27, 1922
WE HAVE PITCHED OUR CAMP NOT FAR FROM AN ENORMOUS SAND DUNE. CONDITIONS ARE EXTREME. ALL THIS SAND IS A FURNACE BY DAY AND A GLACIER AT NIGHT. WE HAVE REDOUBLED OUR EFFORTS. YESTERDAY, WE FOUND THE REMAINS OF A SMALL DINOSAUR, WHICH HAS BEEN NAMED *PROTOCERATOPS*.

FEBRUARY 15, 1923
A DIFFICULT WEEK. THE LAST FEW NIGHTS, OUR TENTS HAVE BEEN INVADED BY VENOMOUS SNAKES! AND AS IF THAT WASN'T ENOUGH, A TERRIBLE SANDSTORM TORE THROUGH THE CAMP YESTERDAY, DESTROYING SOME OF OUR EQUIPMENT. THE TEAM'S MORALE IS AT ITS LOWEST EBB, AND I AM STARTING TO THINK THE DESERT IS DETERMINED TO PROTECT ITS ANCIENT TREASURES.

JULY 5, 1923
FINALLY WE'VE HAD SOME LUCK! A CHINESE PALEONTOLOGIST HERE WITH US HAS UNEARTHED A GIGANTIC MAMMAL SKULL. GIVEN THE SIZE OF ITS JAWBONE, I DREAD TO THINK WHAT THIS CREATURE LOOKED LIKE.

ANDREWSARCHUS
THE ENIGMATIC CARNIVORE

The only evidence that *Andrewsarchus* existed is the skull found by Roy Chapman Andrews on his Gobi Desert expedition. This made reconstructing the animal complicated, and its form remains unclear to this day.

Paleontologists compared this skull to that of a related animal, *Mesonyx*, and decided that *Andrewsarchus* was a gigantic wolf, as long as a large vehicle. For several decades, *Andrewsarchus* was claimed as the largest carnivorous mammal of all time. Recent studies put this terrifying picture into perspective.

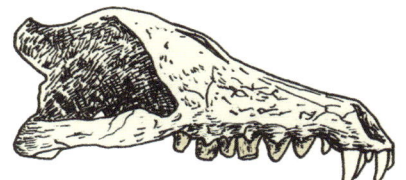

- Found in Mongolia (1923)
- Up to 3–4 m long
- Lived 48 to 37 million years ago

A BIG BAD WOLF OR A GIANT PIG?
While *Andrewsarchus* was long considered to be an ancestor of whales and hippopotami, paleontologists today see it more as a great-aunt or uncle of ancient pigs. The old idea of a large wolf changes into something a little different…

CARNIVORE OR OMNIVORE?
Studies of the teeth of *Andrewsarchus* suggest that it did not just eat meat. It was quite likely an omnivore that also ate roots and shellfish.

WHAT ANIMALS ROAMED THE BADLANDS LONG, LONG AGO?

THE LAKOTA OF NORTH AMERICA TELL STORIES ABOUT THE THUNDER BEASTS WHO COME OUT OF THE SKIES DURING STORMS.

IN THE STORIES, THE THUNDER BEASTS LIVE IN THE SKY AND SOMETIMES COME DOWN TO EARTH TO HUNT BISON. A DEAFENING THUNDERING IS HEARD AS THEY RACE ACROSS THE CLOUDS. THE CLASH OF THEIR HOOVES ON THE EARTH STRIKE SPARKS THAT LIGHT UP THE STORMY SKIES.

WHEN THE HUNT AND THE STORM ARE OVER, THE THUNDER BEASTS SINK INTO THE EARTH WHERE THEIR BONES TURN TO STONE. ALL THE RAIN LOOSENS EARTH IN THE HILLS AND CANYONS, BRINGING BONES TO THE SURFACE.

SOMETIMES PEOPLE WOULD FIND THESE STONE BONES. THEY WERE UNLIKE THE BONES OF ANY LIVING ANIMALS.

WHEN OTHNIEL CHARLES MARSH ARRIVED IN THE BADLANDS IN LAKOTA TERRITORY, HE HEARD ABOUT THESE STORIES AND OF THE LARGE BONES DISCOVERED AFTER THE STORMS. HE WAS SHOWN AN IMPRESSIVE JAWBONE FOSSIL BY SOME LAKOTA. LAKOTA LEADERS WERE DIVIDED ABOUT WHETHER TO LET MARSH LOOK FOR MORE FOSSILS ON THEIR LAND.

MARSH DIDN'T WAIT FOR PERMISSION FROM THE LAKOTA BUT RAN OFF AT NIGHT TO DIG UP FOSSILS, WHICH HE TOOK BACK TO YALE UNIVERSITY. MARSH AND HIS TEAM MANAGED TO RECONSTRUCT A WHOLE ANIMAL. TO CLASSIFY THIS LARGE CREATURE, HE CREATED A NEW ANIMAL FAMILY. MARSH NAMED IT **BRONTOTHERIIDAE**, MEANING "THUNDER BEASTS," AFTER THE LAKOTA STORIES.

MEGACEROPS
HOOVES OF THUNDER

Whenever a paleontologist discovers a new extinct species, they give it a scientific name and have the discovery validated by other scientists. But sometimes several paleontologists are convinced that they discovered and named the animal first, so the same animal ends up with many names. This happened with **Megacerops**, a giant herbivore that roamed the plains and forests of America more than 30 million years ago. In the 20th century, the animal was given various descriptive names: "face of thunder" (*Brontops*) and "titanic beast" (*Titanotherium*). Today's paleontologists use the name **Megacerops** ("large-horned face") from its discovery in 1870. But Othniel Charles Marsh's name *Brontotherium*, "thunder beast," from the 1880s is still popular.

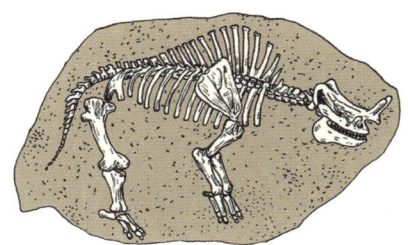

- Found in the United States of America (1870)
- Up to 4.5 m long
- Lived 38 to 34 million years ago

CURIOUS PROTUBERANCES
The fossilized skull of *Megacerops* has bony outgrowths on its nose. These were probably covered in thick skin and were more like the ossicones of a giraffe than the horns of a rhinoceros.

A DECEPTIVE APPEARANCE
Although *Megacerops* resembled a gigantic rhino with thick skin and what looked like a horn, it is actually more closely related to horses.

HOW LONG DID IT TAKE TO UNCOVER THE BEHEMOTH OF THE LOST VALLEY?

IN 1910, THE BRITISH PALEONTOLOGIST SIR CLIVE FORSTER-COOPER EXCAVATED THE FOSSILS OF AN UNKNOWN MAMMAL IN A DESERT IN BALOCHISTAN, PAKISTAN. BASED ON THE APPEARANCE AND SIZE OF SOME BONES, THE CREATURE SEEMED LIKE A GIANT HORNLESS RHINOCEROS.

THE FEW FOSSILS HE TOOK BACK TO ENGLAND GAVE ONLY A SKETCHY PICTURE OF THE CREATURE. BUT BACK IN BALOCHISTAN, SEVERAL WARS IN THE AREA MEANT NO FOSSIL COLLECTING. FOR SEVERAL DECADES IT WAS IMPOSSIBLE TO LEARN MORE ABOUT THIS ANIMAL FROM ANCIENT TIMES.

EIGHTY YEARS LATER, FRENCH PALEONTOLOGIST JEAN-LOUP WELCOMME WENT IN SEARCH OF THE FOSSIL AREA UNCOVERED BY FORSTER-COOPER. WELCOMME AND HIS TEAM DIDN'T HAVE A PRECISE MAP BUT THEY DID GET THE HELP OF THE BUGTI PEOPLE WHO LIVED IN THE SAME TERRITORY. TOGETHER THEY REDISCOVERED THE SPOT IN THE VALLEY AND UNEARTHED AN ALMOST ENTIRE SKELETON. THEN BEGAN THE PATIENT WORK OF RECONSTRUCTION...

PARACERATHERIUM
THE LAST OF THE GIANTS

Thanks to the recent rediscovery of the fossils of this hornless cousin to the rhino, we know much more about *Paraceratherium* today. French paleontologists reconstructed its skeleton by assembling the numerous bones like a puzzle.

Paraceratherium may well have been the largest land mammal of all time. Laboratory studies have gradually brought the animal back to life: using computer drawings and models, paleontologists and paleoartists have been able to picture the creature's likely shape and how it moved.

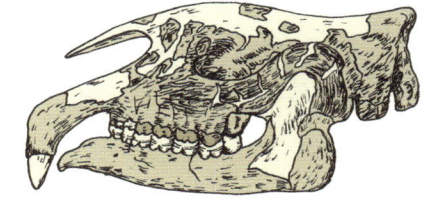

- Found in Pakistan (1908)
- 6 m tall
- Lived 34 to 22 million years ago

SEVERAL NAMES FOR A SINGLE ANIMAL
When Clive Forster-Cooper uncovered a huge skull in 1913, he thought he had discovered a new species and he named it *Baluchitherium*. But about 30 years ago, paleontologists noticed that the species had already been discovered and named in 1908. Today the animal goes by its original name: *Paraceratherium*.

A GRABBING LIP
The shape of *Paraceratherium*'s fossilized skull suggests that the animal had a very flexible top lip, as do rhinos and tapirs, its distant descendants. Its flexible lip was used to grab grass and leaves.

A BRIEF HISTORY OF PALEONTOLOGY

Paleontology is the study of living creatures from the past based on their fossilized remains. This timeline shows how the science of paleontology has progressed. It includes reconstructions of these lost animals, along with the changing beliefs and theories, mistakes and corrections, that have brought our knowledge to where it is today.

ANTIQUITY (5TH CENTURY)
Many texts from ancient times describe prints of fish and shells found in stones. Writers like Xenophanes of Colophon and Pythagoras thought that these were traces of animals living when the sea covered the mountains.

END OF THE 13TH CENTURY
To explain the presence of fossils in mountain stones, a monk called Restoro d'Arezzo said that the flood described in Genesis in the Bible would have carried the shells there. This seemed the only possible explanation in a time and place when the Bible was a very important book to many people.

1809
Professor Jean-Baptiste Lamarck's book *Zoological Philosophy* presented the idea that animals change over time. Arguing with Georges Cuvier, he claimed that species did not become extinct but instead somehow changed over the course of geological time.

MIDDLE AGES
Fossils are associated with all kinds of beliefs (see p.20) during the Middle Ages and the Renaissance. Besides the great flood theory, some scholars believed that fossils were mysteriously produced by the stones themselves.

1796
Scientist Georges Cuvier compared bone fossils like those of **Mosasaurus** (p.49) with the skeletons of current species. He showed their differences and proposed the idea that some animal species had become extinct. A few years later, he explained his theory of catastrophism, which says that certain species have disappeared because of disasters. This is the birth of paleontology as a scientific discipline.

1821
Mary Anning discovered the fossil of a **Plesiosaurus** in 1821 (see p.28). The study of these bones, particularly by Georges Cuvier, confirmed the idea that some species had indeed become extinct. Anning was one of the many amateurs whose discoveries contributed to the rise of paleontology.

1824
From various fossilized fragments, and a piece of jawbone in particular, William Buckland described an extinct giant lizard, which he named *Megalosaurus* ("large lizard"). This was the first description of what British paleontologist Richard Owen would call a "dinosaur" 18 years later.

1842
The term *Dinosauria* was proposed by Richard Owen to bring together three types of large animal discovered in fossil form in England (*Megalosaurus*, **Iguanodon**, p.37, and *Hylaeosaurus*). The name combined two Greek words: *deinos*, "fearsomely large" and *sauros*, "lizard."

1851
The first sculptures of dinosaurs were produced by sculptor Benjamin Waterhouse Hawkins, under the guidance of paleontologist Richard Owen (p.36). Their exhibition in England began the first "dinomania."

1859
Darwin published his book *On the Origin of Species*, in which he explained the evolution of species through natural selection. This theory overturned the long-established classifications of the time. Now animals were grouped by their common ancestors rather than by how they looked. After this, paleontology continued to provide new evidence that new species develop from old ones.

1861
The first **Archaeopteryx** specimen (p.31) was discovered in quarries in Bavaria. As scientists studied this fossil through the 20th century they would see the connection between dinosaurs and birds, the changes between different species, and evidence of evolution.

1877
Othniel Charles Marsh discovered **Stegosaurus** (p.35) in the United States during the bone wars. At the end of the 19th century, this rush for dinosaur fossils would lead to many species being unearthed. As people heard more about these finds, they became more fascinated with the distant past.

1908
The cast of the **Diplodocus** fossil was shown in the paleontology gallery of Paris's natural history museum (see p.32). At the same time, other copies of **Diplodocus** fossils were offered to museums around the world. "Dinomania" went global.

1909
Charles Walcott made the first discovery of fossils dating from the Cambrian period in the Burgess mountains in Canada (see p.16).

1912
The Lost World was published, a novel by Sir Arthur Conan Doyle, author of the famous Sherlock Holmes adventures. The book was popular because many people were interested in dinosaurs at the start of the 20th century. It would inspire many movie versions.

1922
Roy Chapman Andrews led his expedition into the Gobi Desert in Mongolia, which turned out to have many fossils. **Protoceratops** (p.43), **Oviraptor** (p.45) and **Andrewsarchus** (p.61) were all found there.

1931
Painter Charles Robert Knight completed a series of 28 mural paintings for a new fossils hall at the natural history museum in Chicago (see p.42). Knight's portraits of **Tyrannosaurus** (p.51), **Diplodocus** (p.33) and **Protoceratops** (p.43) strongly affected how people saw these animals.

1947
Fossils more than 550 million years old were discovered in ancient mines in Australia. They provided precious evidence for the existence of ancient creatures from Ediacara, including **Dickinsonia** (p.15).

1966
An expedition returned to the Burgess site. The fossils discovered by Charles Walcott were re-examined. New animals from the Cambrian such as **Anomalocaris** (p.17) and **Hallucigenia** (p.19) were described.

1969
American paleontologist John Ostrom published an article describing **Deinonychus** (p.41). His depiction of the animal changed the image of dinosaurs, making **Deinonychus** fast and agile. His work was the starting point for the "dinosaur renaissance" that sparked new interest in these large extinct reptiles.

1991
The Chicxulub crater was discovered in Mexico. Scientists presented this as evidence that Earth was hit by a giant meteorite 66 million years ago. This collision was largely responsible for the extinction of the big dinosaurs (see p.54).

1993
Steven Spielberg's Hollywood movie *Jurassic Park* was released—to huge success—featuring dinosaurs based on the work begun by John Ostrom. *Velociraptor* (inspired by the reconstruction of **Deinonychus** a couple of decades earlier) and **Tyrannosaurus** wowed audiences and became the new stars from the long ago past.

1995
The Messel Pit in Germany was classified a UNESCO World Heritage Site. Because the fossils were in such good shape, this quarry was a goldmine for paleontologists. Its fossils give an accurate picture of the animals of the Palaeogene period, **Propalaeotherium** (p.59) among them.

1996
In China's Liaoning province, the discovery of *Sinosauropteryx* was the first in a long series of fossil finds in this region of feathered dinosaurs such as **Microraptor** (p.39). By studying these fossils, paleontologists would reconstruct the history of the transition between dinosaurs and birds. This revolution put feathers onto dinosaurs like **Deinonychus** (p.41) and **Oviraptor** (p.45).

2004
In northern Canada the fossil of **Tiktaalik** (p.23) was unearthed. Like **Archaeopteryx**, this discovery shed light on the process of evolution—in this case, from fish to tetrapods, four-footed vertebrates.

2008
Fossils were found that were 2.1 billion years old in sediments in Gabon, Africa. This discovery indicated that complex multicellular life had originated 1.5 billion years earlier than previously thought (see p.14). Scientists began to rewrite the history of life on Earth.

2011
Paris's natural history museum acquired an X-ray scanner. By capturing images through stone, the "CT scan" made it possible to see 3D images of fossils within their rocks and to explore their internal anatomy without destroying them. Now paleontologists could see things that had been hidden before.

2017
Patagotitan mayorum ("titan of Patagonia") was described. This Argentinian sauropod is the largest dinosaur discovered so far. It is closely related to *Argentinosaurus* and slightly larger.

The dates listed under fossil illustrations on each righthand page are the date the fossil was described and named.